So You Want A Perfect Wife!

Can you imagine the ecstatic feeling you would have if your wife came up to you and asked, "How can I become a better wife?" The honor you would feel would be overwhelming. Of course, it would be absurd to expect this kind of question to come up between most husbands and wives. But just close your eyes for a moment, lean back in your chair, and picture your wife asking you such a question.

Also by Gary Smalley

FOR BETTER OR FOR BEST

Published by
HARPERPAPERBACKS

IF
ONLY
HE KNEW

BY GARY SMALLEY

HarperPaperbacks
A Division of HarperCollinsPublishers

The stories in this book are true. The names have been changed except for references to the author.

HarperPaperbacks   *A Division of* HarperCollins*Publishers*
10 East 53rd Street, New York, N.Y. 10022

This book is published by arrangement with Zondervan Publishing House.

Unless otherwise indicated, Scripture is from the *New American Standard Bible*, copyright © 1960, 1962, 1963, 1968, 1971, 1972 by The Lockman Foundation.

First HarperPaperbacks printing: June 1991

Manufactured in the United Kingdom by HarperCollins*Publishers* Ltd.

HarperPaperbacks and colophon are trademarks of HarperCollins*Publishers*

10 9 8 7

To the number one woman in my life,
Norma Jean,
and to our children,
Kari, Greg, and Michael

Special Thanks

For those who helped with the first edition:

Bonney Scott:

For her loving commitment, which made the scheduled completion of this book possible.

Robert J. Marsh:

For his vision and encouragement, without which this book would not have been written for at least three years.

The Principals of R.M. Marketing:

For their courage in committing the financial resources that made our dream a reality.

Harry Howard:

For coordinating the layout and physical production of this book.

The Editorial Staff:

Judy Baggett Thrasher and Linda Allen Fyke for enabling us to complete a two-year project in two months.

The Typists:

Anna Ruth Hart, Betty Snyder, Lisa Bland, Darlene Williams, Janet Perry, and Denise Duck for working your fingers to the bone.

Contents

A Note From the Author's Wife

In our continuing work with couples, Gary and I have come to one conclusion: There is no such thing as a unique problem. In fact, most couples are usually relieved to know their problems are common to many, if not all, couples. Because marital problems can be so similar, if you find a solution that works with several couples, it usually will be effective for most couples.

Please rest assured that you are not the first husband in the history of humanity to experience the problems you are facing. The principles that Gary shares in this book have not only made our marriage more fulfilling, but they have had similar results in the lives of countless other couples with whom we have worked. As you begin to apply these principles to your relationship, you should begin to experience a deeper and richer marriage.

Norma Smalley

1

How To Drive
Your Wife Away
Without Even Trying

"You husbands likewise, live with your wives in an understanding way."

1 Peter 3:7

At the other end of the phone a quivering voice said,
"You've got to help me. She has a court order against me."
George was coming to me for help after his relationship
with his wife was already in shreds. "We've been married
over twenty years, and she won't even let me back in the
house. I can't believe she would treat me this way after all
I've done for her. Can you help us get back together?"

Before I answered his question, I wanted to talk to his
wife. "There's no way you can talk to Barbara," he said.
"She wouldn't talk to you. The moment you say you're
representing me in any way, she'll hang up on you."

"I've never been turned down by a wife yet," I assured
him, "so we might as well see if this will be the first time.
Would you give me her phone number?"

To be honest, as grim as things sounded, I did wonder
if she would be the first wife not willing to talk to me about
her marital strife. But my doubts were unfounded—she was
more than anxious to discuss their problems.

"What would it take for you to be willing to let your husband back into your life? What would have to happen before you would try to rebuild a marriage relationship with him?" Those were the same questions I had asked many wives who claimed they didn't want their husbands back.

Her response was typical. "I can't possibly answer that question. He's the worst husband in the world, so I wouldn't think of taking him back. I can't stand his personality or his offensive habits any more." The court order would take care of him, she told me. "Just keep him away!"

I gently asked her if she could tell me the things he had done to offend her. When I heard her response, I said, "It sounds like he hasn't been a very sensitive and gentle husband, has he?"

Once again I asked her to stretch her imagination and think about what changes would be necessary before she would take him back.

There was plenty of room for improvement, she told me. First, he was too domineering and critical of her. Second, he tried to control her every move with a possessive grip. Third, he trampled her sense of self-worth with constant ridicule. And fourth, although he always had time for business and other interests, he seldom took time to listen to her. On top of all that, he spied on her and didn't give her any freedom.

"Don't get any ideas, though," she told me at the end of our conversation. "Because no matter what, I won't stop the divorce."

When I relayed these complaints to George, I knew I had touched some sensitive spots. He defended himself and accused her. I let him rant for a while before asking, "Do you want your wife back?"

"Yes, I'd do anything to get her back," he said.

"Good. I'm always willing to work with someone ready

to readjust his life. But if you're not totally serious, let me know now. I don't like to play games." Again he committed himself to change, but his commitment didn't last beyond my next statement. "We're going to have to work on your domineering and possessive nature. It shows you don't genuinely love your wife."

He fumed and spouted, defended and fought so much I began to wonder if he really would commit himself to the necessary changes.

"I've never met a more belligerent, stubborn man in my entire life!" I exclaimed.

Suddenly subdued, he responded, "That's not my nature. I'm usually rather submissive inside. Maybe I'm putting up a front because I'm really not a pushy person. I feel like people run all over me."

"I don't think you and I are talking about the same person," I responded. "If I were your wife, I'm not sure I could bear up emotionally under your domineering personality."

That stopped him long enough for him to give our conversation some serious thought. After talking to his friends and even praying that God would help him understand, he returned to my office, able to confess his faults and ready to change.

"If you really want to love your wife, then you need to begin right now, at the divorce trial," I said. Now that we were on the subject, he mentioned that he needed to get a lawyer because she had one.

"No," I cautioned him. "If you want to win her back, you need to forget about a lawyer this time." (I don't always recommend this, but based on their personal background, I felt he would stand a better chance of regaining her love without legal counsel.)

"You're crazy," he said. "They'll take me to the cleaners."

Feeling somewhat defenseless, he reluctantly agreed to forfeit legal counsel.

Two of his friends and I waited in the courthouse for the closed-room session to end. He came running out of the courtroom bellowing. "She wants 20% of my retirement . . . 20%! No way I'm gonna do that!"

Once again I asked him, "Do you want your wife back?" Again, he nodded yes! " Then give her 25%." I reminded him that *now* was the time to respect her and treat her sensitively. Later, he emerged from the courtroom a divorced man, but not for long. . . .

Several months later I ran into him at the grocery store. "My wife and I remarried," he said triumphantly. "I thought you were crazy when you first told me the things I should do for my wife . . . there was no way I would ever be able to do them," he continued. "It took sheer will power at first. I only did them because you said that God rewards those who seek Him and follow His ways. But you know, it's really amazing. After doing them for three months, I actually enjoy them."

He continued to give examples of the new ways he was treating his wife. Like the time she took a business trip and he wrote her a note telling her how much he wished he could be with her. Inserted in the note were extra money and directions on how to reach her destination.

George has finally realized that his wife is a special person who needs tender treatment, almost as if her forehead were stamped "Very Important—Handle With Care"!

He has discovered the secret to renewing any strained relationship—honor. This is discussed further in chapter 3; before we discuss rebuilding a failing marriage, let's examine two major reasons marriages fail.

TWO REASONS MARRIAGES FAIL

1. *Men and women enter marriage with "storybook" expectations and limited training.*

I once asked a college girl what kind of man she would like to marry. "I'd like for him to be able to tell jokes, sing and dance, and stay home at night."

"You don't want a husband," I told her. "You want a television set."

Her visions of a husband reveal one of the most common reasons marriages fail. We marry with unrealistic expectations and few, if any, caring skills. In fact, most of us are rather fuzzy when it comes to our mates' real needs.

Isn't it ironic that a plumber's license requires four years of training, but a marriage license requires nothing but two willing bodies and sometimes a blood test? Since most of us bounce through the educational corridors without any basic communication courses, many men marry with absolutely no knowledge of how to build a meaningful relationship. In short, most men have no idea how to love their wives in a way that makes both of them happy.

Recently I asked five divorced women, individually, "If your husband began treating you in a consistently loving manner, would you take him back?"

"Of course I would," each replied. But, unfortunately, none had hope that her husband would ever be like that.

Because I knew one of the men personally, I had to concur with his wife's hopelessness. If he were willing to try, he could win her back. Unfortunately, he wasn't interested in learning.

"What he doesn't realize is that a lot of women are as responsive as puppies," one woman explained to me. "If he'd come back and treat me with tenderness, gentleness, and understanding, I'd take him back tomorrow."

How sad that we men don't know how to win our wives back or even how to keep from losing them. How can we win their affection, their respect, their love and cooperation when *we don't even know where to begin?* Instead of trying to learn what it takes to mend a cracked marriage, most of us would rather jump on the divorce bandwagon.

We violate the relationship laws inherent in marriage, and then we wonder why it all goes sour. But we wouldn't wonder if the law of aerodynamics sent a one-winged airplane plummeting to the earth.

Imagine yourself an aerospace engineer working for NASA. Your job is to put several men on the moon, but something goes wrong halfway through their flight. You wouldn't dream of walking out on the entire project because something went wrong. Instead, you and the other engineers would put your heads together, insert data into the computer, and . . . violà! You would work night and day to try to discover the problem and make all the vital adjustments to get that spacecraft back on course or help the men return to earth. If the project had failed altogether, you still wouldn't forsake it. You would study what happened and modify it to avoid similar problems in the future.

Like the spacecraft, your marriage is subject to laws that determine its success or failure. If any of these laws are violated, you and your wife are locked into orbits, destined to crash. However, if during the marriage you recognize which law or principle you are violating and make the necessary adjustments, your marriage will stay on the right course.

---

2. *Men and women lack understanding about the general differences between men and women.*

I would venture to say that most marital difficulties center around one fact—men and women are TOTALLY different. The differences (emotional, mental, and physical) are so extreme that without a *concentrated effort* to understand them, it is nearly impossible to have a happy marriage. A famous psychiatrist once said, "After thirty years of studying women, I ask myself, 'What is it that they really want?'" If this was his conclusion, just imagine how little we know about our wives.

You may already be aware of some of the differences. Many, however, will come as a complete surprise. Did you know, for instance, that virtually every cell in a man's body has a chromosome makeup entirely different from those in a woman's body? How about this next one? Dr. James Dobson says there is strong evidence indicating that the "seat" of the emotions in a man's brain is wired differently than in a woman's. By virtue of these two differences alone, men and women are miles apart emotionally and physically. Let's examine some of the differences between men and women.

MENTAL/EMOTIONAL DIFFERENCES

1. Women tend to be more *personal* than men. Women have a deeper interest in people and feelings—building relationships—while men tend to be more preoccupied with practicalities that can be understood through logical deduction. Men tend to be more conquer oriented—competing for dominance—hence, their strong interest in sports such as football and boxing.

Why would a woman be less interested in a boxing match? Because close, loving relationships are usually not developed in the ring! Also, watch what happens during many family vacations. He is challenged by the goal of driving four hundred miles a day, while she wants to stop now and then to drink coffee and relax and relate. He thinks that's a waste of time because it would interfere with his goal.

Men tend to be less desirous and knowledgeable in building intimate relationships, both with women and with others. For example, women are usually the ones who buy marriage books. They are usually the ones who develop the initial interest in knowing God and attending church. When a man realizes that his wife is more naturally motivated to nurture relationships, he can relax and accept these tendencies and *choose* to develop a better marriage and better relationships with his children.

As a husband, do you realize that your wife's natural ability for developing relationships can actually *help* you fulfill the two greatest commandments taught by Christ—loving God and loving others (Matt. 22:36–40)? Jesus said that if we obey these two commandments, we are fulfilling *all* the commandments. Think of it! Your wife has the God-given drive and ability to help you build meaningful relationships in both these areas. God knew you needed special help because He stated, "It is not good for the man to be alone; I will make him a helper [and completer] suitable for him" (Gen. 2:18). If you let her, your wife can open up a whole new and complete world of communication and deeper relationships.

2. Women become an intimate part of their surroundings. Dr. Cecil Osborne, in his book *The Art of Understanding Your Mate*, said women become *an intimate part of* the people they know and the things that surround them; they enter into a kind of "oneness" with their environment. Though a man relates to people and situations, he usually doesn't allow his identity to become entwined with them. He somehow remains apart. That's why a woman, viewing her house

as an extension of herself, can be hurt when it's criticized by others. A man may not realize it, but when he yells at the kids for something they did, his words affect her deeply as well.

Women tend to find their identity in close relationships, while men gain their identity through vocations.

3. Women often need more time to adjust to change. Because of a woman's *emotional identity* with people and places around her, she needs more time to adjust to change that may affect her relationships. A man can logically deduce the benefits of a change and get "psyched-up" for it in a matter of minutes. Not so with a woman. Since she focuses on immediate consequences of relocating, for example, she needs time to overcome the initial adjustment before warming up to the advantages of it.

4. Women tend to express their hostility *verbally* whereas men tend to be more *physically* violent.

PHYSICAL DIFFERENCES

Dr. Paul Popenoe, founder of the American Institute of Family Relations in Los Angeles, dedicated his most productive years to the research of biological differences between the sexes. Some of his findings are listed below.

- Woman has greater constitutional vitality, perhaps because of her unique chromosome makeup. Normally, female outlives male by four to eight years in the U.S.
- Woman's metabolism is normally lower than man's.
- Man and woman differ in skeletal structure, woman having a shorter head, broader face, less protruding chin, shorter legs, and longer trunk.

- Woman has larger kidneys, liver, stomach, and appendix than man, but smaller lungs.
- Woman has several unique and important functions: menstruation, pregnancy, lactation. Woman's hormones are of a different type and more numerous than man's.
- Woman's thyroid is larger and more active. It enlarges during pregnancy and menstruation; makes woman more prone to goiter; provides resistance to cold; is associated with her smooth-skinned, relatively hairless body and thin layer of subcutaneous fat.
- Woman's blood contains more water and 20 percent fewer red cells. Since the red cells supply oxygen to the body cells, woman tires more easily and is more prone to faint. Her constitutional vitality is, therefore, limited to "life span." (When the working day in British factories was increased from ten to twelve hours under wartime conditions, accidents increased 150 percent among women but not at all among men.)
- On the average, man possesses 50 percent more brute strength than woman (40 percent of a man's body weight is muscle; 23 percent of a woman's).
- Woman's heart beats more rapidly (average 80 beats per minute vs. 72 for man). Woman's blood pressure (10 points lower than man's) varies from minute to minute, but she has less tendency toward high blood pressure—at least until after menopause.
- Woman's vital capacity or breathing power is significantly lower than man's.
- Woman withstands high temperatures better than man because her metabolism slows down less.

SEXUAL DIFFERENCES

A woman's sexual drive tends to be related to her menstrual cycle, while a man's drive is fairly constant. The hormone testosterone is a major factor in stimulating a man's sexual desire.

A woman is stimulated more by touch and romantic words. She is far more attracted by a man's personality, while the man is stimulated by sight. A man is usually less discriminating about those to whom he is physically attracted.

While a man needs little or no preparation for sex, a woman often needs hours of emotional and mental preparation. Harsh or abusive treatment can easily remove her desire for sexual intimacy for days at a time. When a woman's emotions have been trampled by her husband, she is often repulsed by his advances. Many women have told me they feel like prostitutes when they're forced to make love while feeling resentment toward their husbands. However, a man may not be AWARE of what he is putting his wife through if she feels he is forcing sex upon her.

These basic differences, which usually surface soon after the wedding, are the source of many conflicts in marriage. From the start, the woman has a greater intuitive awareness of how to develop a loving relationship. Because of her sensitivity, she is initially more considerate of his feelings and enthusiastic about developing a meaningful, multilevel relationship: that is, she knows how to build something more than a sexual marathon; she wants to be a lover, a best friend, a fan, a homemaker, and an appreciated partner. The man, on the other hand, does not generally have her instinctive awareness of what the relationship should

11

be. He doesn't know how to encourage and love his wife or treat her in a way that meets her deepest needs.

Since he doesn't have an understanding of these vital areas through intuition, he must rely *solely* upon the knowledge and skills he has acquired *prior* to marriage. Unfortunately, our educational system does not require a training program for a husband-to-be. His only education may be the example he observed in his home. For many of us, that example may have been insufficient. We enter marriage knowing everything about sex and very little about genuine, unselfish love.

I am not saying men are more selfish than women. I'm simply saying that at the outset of a marriage most men are not as equipped to express unselfish love or as desirous of nurturing marriage into a loving and lasting relationship as women are.

INTUITIVE DIFFERENCES

Norman was planning to invest more than $50,000 in a business opportunity that was a "sure thing." He had scrutinized it from every angle and had logically deduced that it couldn't miss. After signing a contract and delivering a check to the other party, he decided to tell his wife about the investment.

Upon hearing a few of the details, she immediately felt uneasy about the deal. Norman sensed her uneasiness and became angry, asking why she felt that way. She couldn't give a logical reason because she didn't have one. All she knew was that it just didn't "sit right." Norman gave in, went back to the other party, and asked for a refund. "You're crazy!" the man told him as he returned Norman's money. A short time later, ALL of the organizers and investors were indicted by the federal government. His wife's intuition had not only saved him $50,000, but it may have kept Norman out of jail.

What exactly is this "woman's intuition"? It's not something mystical. According to a Stanford University research team led by neuropsychologists McGuinness and Tribran, women do catch subliminal messages faster and more accurately than men. Since this intuition is based on an unconscious mental process, many women aren't able to give specific explanations for the way they feel. They simply perceive or "feel" something about a situation or person, while men tend to follow a logical analysis of circumstances or people.

Now that you know several reasons why men and women cannot understand their respective differences without great effort, I hope you will have more hope, patience, and tolerance as you endeavor to strengthen and deepen your relationship with your wife. With this in mind, let's look at some of the serious consequences of allowing a poor marriage to continue in its downhill slide.

SERIOUS CONSEQUENCES OF A POOR MARRIAGE

First, a woman who is not properly loved by her husband can develop any number of serious physical ailments needing thousands of dollars' worth of treatment, according to Dr. Ed Wheat, a noted Christian physician.

Second, every aspect of a woman's emotional and physical existence is dependent on the romantic love she receives from her husband, says Dr. James Dobson. So, husbands, if *you* feel locked out of your bedroom, listen closely. According to Dr. Dobson, when a man learns to love his wife in the way she needs to be loved, she will respond to him physically in a way he never dreamed possible.

Third, a husband's lack of love for his wife can drastically affect their children's emotional development, according to John Drescher in his book, *Seven Things Children Need*.

Fourth, a disrespectful wife and rebellious children are more likely to be found in the home of a man who does not know how to lovingly support his family.

Fifth, when a man settles for a poor marriage, he is forfeiting his reputation before all the world. He is saying, "I don't care what I promised at the marriage altar; I'm not going to try any longer." By refusing to love his wife as he should, he is telling those around him that he is self-centered and unreliable.

Sixth, the son of an unloving husband will probably learn many of the wrong ways to treat his future wife by modeling after his father. Unloving parents simply can't keep their problems to themselves. They are bound to affect their children's future relationships.

And seventh, improper love increases the possibility of mental illness requiring psychiatric treatment of family members. Echoing what the Bible said centuries ago, Dr. Nathan Ackerman in an article in *Family Weekly*, said mental illness is passed on within a family, transmitted from generation to generation. In that same article, Dr. Salvador Minuchin, a psychiatrist, said family members often get caught in a groove of mental illness by putting undue stress on each other.

THE HARDEST DECISION YOU MAY EVER MAKE

I am not trying to force you into the "perfect husband" mold. I don't know *any* perfect husbands. However, I do know some who are learning how to respond to their wives' special needs.

What I do want to do is to help you learn how to love your wife more effectively and consistently. At first you may feel like you're learning to walk all over again. Weeks, months, or even a year may pass before you reach your goal of consistent loving behavior. After you learn to make progress, you will gain confidence. Soon you will be right in the midst of the kind of marriage you never thought possible.

Remember—you may feel it's impossible to change life-long habits, but it's not. It usually takes from thirty to sixty days to change a habit. So I hope you will decide to try to change yours. For some men it may take the accountability of a small group or the support of a pastor. However, I know from experience that the rewards are well worth the effort.

The Secret to a Fulfilling Marriage

Persistence!! Sometimes in the middle of a conflict with Norma I really want to give up. But that's only how I felt. Often I'm tired, run down, under too much stress—consequently, the future looks bleak. That's when I rely upon knowledge, not feelings. I act upon what *will* strengthen our relationship, and in a few days I see the results. In fact, I usually feel better the next day and have renewed desire to work on our marriage. So *I never give up*. I keep acting on what I've learned from the Bible are the secrets of lasting relationships.

I act on those secrets no matter how I feel. I've tried to expand and illustrate those secrets throughout this book.

Remember, *you* are the one who gains when you strive to have a loving relationship with your wife. My wife has told me dozens of times that when I treat her right I'm the one who wins. My loving care motivates her to do extra things for me, to respond gladly to my needs and desires, but this has never been my main motivation. The strongest motivation for me has been the *challenge* and *rewards* of living my life as outlined in Scripture. For me, it's following the two greatest teachings of Christ—to know and love God and to know and love people (Matt. 22:36–40). All the joy and fulfillment I have desired in this life have come from these two relationships—with God and with others (Eph. 3:19–20; John 15:11–13). These relationships are so important that I have added to my own life another motivation—perhaps the best motivation for me. I allow a few other couples to hold me accountable for loving my wife and children. They have the freedom to ask me how we're doing, as a couple and as a family, and I know they love me enough to lift me up when I fall. And I always try to remember that love is a *choice*. I choose to care about my relationships. That same choice leading to great rewards can be yours.

My wife and I have committed the remaining years of our lives to the study of skills needed to rebuild meaningful relationships. I have personally interviewed hundreds of women about what actions of their husbands tear down or build up their marriages. Basically, this book is a summary of my findings. (Even now, we're in the process of researching and discovering what it takes to motivate men relationally and why men tend to resist growth in this area. Our goal once we isolate these key factors is to call 100,000 men, nationwide, to an all-out commitment to their families.)

Your wife may be a career woman without children or a busy homemaker and mother of three. Whatever the case, I believe you can *customize* the general principles in this book to build a more fulfilling relationship with her.

Before reading the next chapter, take this short quiz to rate how stable your marriage is at this moment. Then, when you have pinpointed your weak and strong points, use the chapters that follow to take steps necessary to strengthen your relationship. Some of the ideas for this checklist are from Dr. George Larson, a psychologist who has done extensive work helping people develop good relationships. He believes, as I do, that good relationships don't just happen. They evolve and are sustained only when people know what they want and how to get it.

Answer YES *or* NO *to each question, then check your score below:*

1. Do you make your wife feel good about herself? (yes ___ no _✓_)
2. Do you value the same things in your wife that you value in yourself? (yes ___ no _✓_)
3. Does your face spontaneously break into a smile when you see your wife? (yes ___ no _✓_)
4. When you leave the house, does your wife have a sense of well-being, having been nourished by your company? (yes ___ no _✓_)
5. Can you and your wife tell each other honestly what you really want instead of using manipulation or games? (yes ___ no _✓_)

6. Can your wife get angry at you without your thinking less of her? (yes ___ no ✓)

7. Can you accept your wife as she is instead of having several plans to redo her? (yes ___ no ___)

8. Is your behavior consistent with your words? (yes ___ no ___)

9. Do your actions show you really care for your wife? (yes ___ no ___)

10. Can you feel comfortable with your wife when she's wearing old clothes? (yes ___ no ___)

11. Do you enjoy introducing your wife to your friends or acquaintances? (yes ___ no ___)

12. Are you able to share with your wife your moments of weakness, failure, disappointment? (yes ___ no ___)

13. Would your wife say you are a good listener? (yes ___ no ___)

14. Do you trust your wife to solve her own problems? (yes ___ no ___)

15. Do you admit to your wife you have problems and need her comfort? (yes ___ no ___)

16. Do you believe you could live a full and happy life without your wife? (yes ___ no ___)

17. Do you encourage your wife to develop her full potential as a woman? (yes ___ no ___)

18. Are you able to learn from your wife and value what she says? (yes ___ no ___)

19. If your wife were to die tomorrow, would you be very happy you had the chance to meet her and to marry her? (yes ___ no ___)

20. Does your wife feel she's more important than anyone or anything else in your life other than God? (yes ___ no ___)

21. Do you believe you know at least five of your wife's

major needs and how to meet those needs in a skillful way? (yes ___ no ___)

22. Do you know what your wife needs when she's under stress or when she's discouraged? (yes ___ no ___)

23. When you offend your wife, do you usually admit you were wrong and seek her forgiveness? (yes ___ no ___)

24. Would your wife say you praise her at least once a day? (yes ___ no ___)

25. Would your wife say you are open to her correction? (yes ___ no ___)

26. Would your wife say you are a protector, that you know what her limitations are as a woman? (yes ___ no ___)

27. Would your wife say you usually consider her feelings and ideas whenever making a decision that affects the family or her? (yes ___ no ___)

28. Would your wife say you enjoy being with her and sharing many of life's experiences with her? (yes ___ no ___)

29. Would your wife say you are a good example of what you would like her to be? (yes ___ no ___)

30. Would you say you create interest in her when you share things you consider important? (yes ___ no ___)

If you answered "yes" to 10 or less questions, then your relationship is in major need of overhaul.

If you answered "yes" to 11–19 of the questions, your relationship needs improvement.

If you answered "yes" to 20 or more, then you're probably on your way to a good, lasting relationship.

FOR PERSONAL REFLECTION

1. What two main responsibilities are required of every husband? 1 Peter 3:7.

2. What is the biblical requirement to love and what do these verses have in common? John 15:13; 1 Corinthians 13:5; Philippians 2:3–8.
3. What do we gain from loving others? John 15:11; Galatians 5:13–14; Ephesians 3:19–20.

2

Where Have All
The Feelings Gone?

"But the greatest of these is love."

1 Corinthians 13:13

"I don't love you any more," Sandi said casually, shocking Jim out of his intense interest in a baseball game on TV. "I want to leave you, and I'm taking Jamey with me," she added. Jim whirled around in his chair, wondering if he had heard correctly.

Since Sandi and Jim believed themselves to be sensible, educated adults, they separated calmly and agreed on a settlement without dispute. Jim, in his "maturity," even helped Sandi pack. Then he calmly watched as she and his daughter left his house for good. But he wasn't calm on the inside. He couldn't keep food down for the next month, and it wasn't long before he developed shingles and boils. His physical problems were only symptoms of a much deeper problem—a lack of *knowledge* and *interest* in building a lasting marriage relationship.

Fortunately, Jim was able to win his wife back with genuine love. It took a year, but Sandi was finally convinced by the changes in Jim that their marriage deserved another try. Jim got a second chance at his marriage. Unfortunately, not all men do.

Just what did Jim learn about love during a year of separation from Sandi? He learned that a successful marriage, like any other worthwhile endeavor, takes time and study.

Who would think of allowing an untrained man to climb into the cockpit of an airplane and tinker with the gauges? Or who would allow a novice to service the engines of a modern jet? Yet we expect men to build strong, loving relationships without any education at all. A man must be "educated": He first must discover the essentials of genuine love, then practice them until his skills are sharp and natural. Soon his awkwardness will give way to masterful ability.

Remember the couple I mentioned in the first chapter? By the time George finally asked me how he could win his wife's love back, she had already obtained a court order to keep him away from the house. The divorce was pending, although he desperately wanted to salvage their marriage of many years. I can remember telling him, "It'll be difficult. But I assure you, as long as she isn't in love with another man, what I'm going to share with you will work."

At first, he felt awkward using the techniques I shared with him. He had to begin at zero and slowly learn to talk to Barbara, to be tender, and to care about and understand her feelings. He didn't know her special needs, that she longed for comfort and not lectures when discouraged. But in time, he DID learn and he DID win back his wife. He said he couldn't believe the gestures that once felt so awkward were now an enjoyable part of his life.

"It's just not worth it," one husband said when I told him how to save his marriage. "Don't you see, I don't like her any more. She bugs me, and I don't even want to make the effort to build what you're talking about. I just want out."

"What's the matter between the two of you?" I asked, trying to find out why his love for her had vanished. "Why can't you extend yourself toward her and try to build a loving relationship? Why don't you want to?"

"Well," he confided, "several things she has done have hurt me so much that I just can't try any more."

The next day at lunch he named seven things his wife had done, and continued to do, that made him feel like leaving. To his amazement, we were able to trace each area he hated in his wife to an area he saw lacking in his own life. Once he understood this, he asked, "What kind of man would I be to dump her when I'm contributing to the way she is?"

A marital relationship that endures and becomes more fulfilling for both the husband and the wife is no accident. Only hard work makes a marriage more fulfilling five, ten, fifteen, or twenty years after the honeymoon. I enjoy my wife's company more than ever, and I'm looking forward to a deeper relationship in later years.

THE THREE ESSENTIAL KINDS OF LOVE

Nearly every man enters marriage believing his love for his mate will never fade. Yet in the U.S., for every two marriages, there is one divorce. Why? Because we have believed in Hollywood's version of love. But it doesn't take long to discover that mere passion, which revolves around sexual gratification, is not sufficient, in itself, to establish a lasting relationship. Unfortunately, too many couples begin their marriages thinking this type of love is all they need.

IF ONLY

There are at least three kinds of love, each totally unique. Of the three—companionship, passion, and genuine love—I believe only the latter provides an adequate foundation for a secure relationship. If a relationship lacks genuine love, it will most likely deteriorate. One of the most exciting virtues of *genuine love* is that it can be developed within your character without the help of affectionate feelings. Before we look at genuine love, let's first consider the other two types of love.

Companionship

Here we're talking about the "I like you" feelings we have toward the opposite sex—the kind of love that pleasantly stimulates all five senses. She smells good, feels good, sounds good, and looks good. She is pleasant company because she makes you feel happy. You love her like you "love pizza" or you "love country and western music."

Many relationships begin with this type of love. We all notice attractive features in others. Soon we find ourselves enjoying the parts of their lives that make us feel good.

Though this love is the foundation for many marriages, it doesn't always withstand the pressure of time. After two or three years, the wife changes her lifestyle and hairdo while her husband opts for a new cologne and different political views. The older they get, the more they change.

We all change to some degree each year. The danger arises when we base our love on changeable characteristics we found attractive on the companionship level. Our feelings grow colder and colder until we finally wonder what we ever liked about our mates in the first place. So we're off to look for someone new to love. It's easy to see why *companionship love* has trouble maturing and lasting over the years.

Passion

Passion works harder on the emotions than companionship. It's the type of love that keeps the heart working overtime: "Hey, you really turn me on!" The Greeks called it eros—a sensual and physical form of love that often produces ardent physical involvement before and after marriage. Eros love heightens our senses and stimulates our bodies and minds. It's the kind of love that hungers for the other person to stimulate and satisfy our sexual urges. This love is certainly found in marriage, but if passion exists without genuine love, usually lust gives way to disgust and repulsion, somewhat as it did with King David's son Amnon who hated Tamar after he raped her (2 Sam. 13:15).

Genuine Love

Genuine love is completely different. It means, "I see a need in you. Let me have the privilege of meeting it." Instead of taking for itself, genuine love gives to others. It motivates us to help others reach their full potential in life.

Most importantly, genuine love has no qualifications. It doesn't say, "I'll be your friend if you'll be mine." Nor does it say, "I want you to be my girlfriend because you are beautiful and I want people to see us together"; nor, "I want to be your friend because your family is rich." This love does not seek to gain, but only to give. Don't you remember those junior-high crushes when you said, "Well, I'll like her if she likes me, but if she gives me a bad time, I'm dumping her." Genuine love has no such "fine print."

THE LOWEST LEVEL OF MATURITY

The ability to love in a selfless way is dependent upon your level of maturity. The emotions listed below are typical of immature love. Check the ones characteristic of your life.

- *Jealousy* is caused by a fear of losing something or someone we value because it or they meet our needs.
- *Envy* springs from a desire to possess what someone else has. We imagine that if we gain what he or she has, then we'll be happy.
- *Anger* results from the inner turmoil and frustration we feel when we cannot control people or circumstances. We cannot have what we believe will make us happy or our goals are blocked.
- *Loneliness* results from a dependence on other people for our happiness.
- *Fear* results when we imagine or perceive that our needs or goals will not be met.

If you want to continue this exercise, you should make a list of incidents that have triggered each emotion you checked. Then ask yourself, "Why did I feel the emotion? Was I focusing on what I could *get* out of life or what I might *lose* in life?"

All these emotions are characteristic of immature love— a desire to use other people for personal happiness, a hunger for pleasure without regard for the cost. This same immaturity is behind the *abuse* of alcohol, drugs, and sex and the weakening of all our relationships.

THE HIGHEST LEVEL OF MATURITY

I believe the more we help others achieve their full potential in life, the closer we are to maturity. Demonstrating a selfless desire for others to gain is the strongest base for building lasting relationships. How can you go wrong when you develop a love that is primarily concerned with discovering what builds a deep and lasting marriage and how to identify your wife's specific needs and then you look for creative ways to meet them?

LEARNING TO DEVELOP A LASTING, MATURE LOVE

What do you think is the major stumbling block for most husbands in developing a lasting love for their mates? I have found that it is failing to meet a woman's needs from her viewpoint.

When Anna told me she felt unloved in special areas, Mike was dumbfounded. "What do you mean?" he asked her.

"Well, for years you have been a great husband and a very helpful person, and you've done a lot of nice things for me," she explained gently. "But sometimes you do things I don't need. I'd appreciate it if you'd find out what is important to *me*."

A man's brilliant idea can backfire. Like the time I decided to have our house painted as a special surprise for my wife. What was special to me wasn't so special to her. Although she appreciated the paint job, she would have much rather had a new kitchen floor. When I realized that, I stopped my projects long enough to buy her a new kitchen floor. Then we made a list of priorities from her point of view. They were quite different from mine!

Doing things for others _our_ way is a selfish, immature form of love. My heart goes out to those wives who have received pool tables for Christmas, tickets for a trip to the fishing swamps of Louisiana, or invitations to the Motor-man's Ball.

If you've never done so, find out what _your wife_ needs to feel fulfilled as a woman. Then look for special ways to fulfill her needs. At first she may not believe your caring attitude will last. Don't despair. It takes a long time to develop a sturdy relationship.

Many wives are cautious at first when they see their mates becoming more caring. Like the husband who heard a lecture on love and marriage and surprised his wife with a box of candy and a dozen roses. "Oh, this is terrible," she said, weeping. "The baby cut his finger, I burned your dinner when I couldn't get rid of the vacuum cleaner salesman, the sink is stopped up . . . and now _you_ come home drunk!"

Don't be surprised if your wife doesn't understand your actions at first. It took at least two years before mine would admit that I really was changing. Now she knows I am committed to spending the rest of my life developing our relationship and meeting her needs.

Learning how to love your wife in a mature way is like raising a productive vegetable garden. If you have ever tried it, you will appreciate the comparison. Our first year in Texas we decided to grow a vegetable garden. After we dug a small plot, I dumped nearly half a bag of fertilizer on it and let it sit for three months to be sure I'd have a lush garden. But something went wrong. When the carrots came up, they were a little brown around the edges. All the tomatoes began to rot on the bottom before they ripened, so we had to pick them while they were green. None of our beans survived above the half-foot level, and our cucumbers bit the dust.

I was truly puzzled until an expert gardener told me I had "burned" my vegetables with too much fertilizer. My intentions were good, but my knowledge was limited. A husband can fail in much the same way if he doesn't know exactly how much of each "love ingredient" his wife needs. In fact, this book was written to give you some very specific guidelines for "growing" a stronger marriage.

I've seen many marriage relationships that looked just like my garden does now: full of weeds and overrun with bermuda grass—neglected. I've often thought how great it would be if vegetables could talk. If only the beans could have said, "Hey, you up there! You put way too much fertilizer in this garden, and we're having a tough time. The chemicals are killing us, and if you don't do something about it, we're all going to die." If my vegetables could talk, I could have the world's greatest garden. Fortunately, my wife can talk. I can ask her just *what* she needs, *how much* she needs, and *when* she needs it.

(Wives, if you are reading this, let me assure you that we as husbands generally *do not* know what you need. So we ask you to help us learn by telling us your needs in a gentle, loving way. Let us know when we aren't meeting your needs—but not in a critical way that could cause us to lose interest.)

Since understanding and meeting your wife's needs is a golden key to a fulfilling marriage, the rest of this book deals with that subject.

Your wife's needs.

I believe a woman needs to be in harmony with her husband through a deep, intimate relationship. She needs comradeship, harmony, and a feeling of togetherness.

To satisfy your wife, I believe you need to make a dedicated effort to meet each of her needs explained below and expanded in later chapters.

1. Your wife needs to feel that she is very valuable in your life, more important than your mother, your children, your friends, your secretary, and your job.
2. When your wife is stressed out and hurting, she needs to know that you are willing to share an intimate moment of comfort without demanding explanations or giving lectures.
3. She needs open or unobstructed communication.
4. She needs to be praised so she can feel a valuable part of your life.
5. She needs to feel free to help you without fearing retaliation and anger.
6. She needs to know that you will defend and protect her.
7. She needs to know that her opinion is so valuable that you will discuss decisions with her, and act only after carefully evaluating her advice.
8. She needs to share her life with you in every area—home, family, and outside interests.
9. She needs you to be the kind of man her son can follow and her daughter would want to marry.
10. She needs to be tenderly held often, just to be near you, apart from times of sexual intimacy.

When her needs are met, a woman gains security and glows with a sense of well-being. Some of her glow will rub off on you, especially if you are responsible for it in the first place.

THREE SAFEGUARDS IN READING THE REST OF THIS BOOK

I hope you will practice these "safeguards" with each chapter you read, since the ideas I put forth are general in nature.

First, discuss each chapter with your wife to see where she agrees and disagrees. Think of her as a flower. All flowers are beautiful, but each needs a specific amount of sunlight, nutrients, and water to flourish. You need to discover who she really is, especially as she changes from year to year.

Second, after she has shared her unique needs, rephrase them in your own words until she says you have picked up her meaning. It is your responsibility to find out what your wife means when she says, "You said you'd be back in a *little while.*" A little while might mean thirty minutes to her and two hours to you.

Third, it is important to remember how much you both differ as male and female. In general, a wife is naturally more sensitive and more aware of relationships than her husband. Try to understand that she will probably feel, see, and hear more than you. When your wife says something to you, allow it to sink in. Make an extra effort to understand your relationship as she sees it.

100 WAYS

The rest of this chapter is devoted to showing you one hundred ways you can love your wife *her way.* Discuss this list with your wife. Ask her to check the ones that are meaningful to her, and then arrange them in order of importance to her. Use the list as a basis for learning her views. I know your relationship will be greatly strengthened as you learn how to use these suggestions:

1. Communicate with her; never close her out.
2. Regard her as important.
3. Do everything you can to understand her feelings.
4. Be interested in her friends.
5. Ask her opinion frequently.
6. Value what she says.
7. Let her feel your approval and affection.
8. Protect her on a daily basis.
9. Be gentle and tender with her.
10. Develop a sense of humor. *Don't have to be born with it*
11. Avoid sudden major changes without discussion and without giving her time to adjust.
12. Learn to respond openly and verbally when she wants to communicate.
13. Comfort her when she is down emotionally. For instance, put your arms around her and silently hold her for a few seconds without lectures or put-downs.
14. Be interested in what she feels is important in life.
15. Correct her gently and tenderly.
16. Allow her to teach you without putting up your defenses.
17. Make special time available to her and your children.
18. Be trustworthy.
19. Compliment her often.
20. Be creative when you express your love, either in words or actions.
21. Have specific family goals for each year.
22. Let her buy things she considers necessary.
23. Be forgiving when she offends you.
24. Show her you need her.

25. Accept her the way she is; discover her uniqueness as special.
26. Admit your mistakes; don't be afraid to be humble.
27. Lead your family in their spiritual relationship with God.
28. Allow your wife to fail; discuss what went wrong, after you have comforted her.
29. Rub her feet or neck after a hard day.
30. Take time for the two of you to sit and talk calmly.
31. Go on romantic outings.
32. Write her a letter occasionally, telling her how much you love her.
33. Surprise her with a card ~~or flowers~~.
34. Express how much you appreciate her.
35. Tell her how proud you are of her.
36. Give advice in a loving way when she asks for it.
37. Defend her to others.
38. Prefer her over others.
39. Do not expect her to do activities beyond her emotional or physical capabilities.
40. Pray for her to enjoy God's best in life.
41. Take time to notice what she has done for you and the family.
42. Brag about her to other people behind her back.
43. Share your thoughts and feelings with her.
44. Tell her about your job if she is interested.
45. Take time to see how she spends her day, at work or at home.
46. Learn to enjoy what she enjoys.
47. Take care of the kids before dinner.
48. Help straighten up the house ~~before mealtime~~.
49. Let her take a bubble bath while you do the dishes.
50. Understand her physical limitations if ~~you have several children~~.

51. Discipline the children [Torrey] in love, not anger.

52. Help her finish her goals—hobbies or education.

53. Treat her as if God had stamped on her forehead, "Handle with care."

54. Get rid of habits that annoy her. !

55. Be gentle and thoughtful to her relatives.

56. Do not compare her relatives with yours in a negative way.

57. Thank her for things she has done without expecting anything in return.

58. Do not expect a band to play whenever you help with the housecleaning.

59. Make sure she understands <u>everything</u> you are planning to do.

60. Do little things for her—an unexpected kiss, coffee in bed.

61. Treat her as an intellectual equal.

62. Find out if she wants to be treated as physically weaker.

63. Discover her fears in life. NOT MAKE FUN OF FEARS

64. See what you can do to eliminate her fears.

65. Discover her sexual needs.

66. Ask if she wants to discuss how you can meet her sexual needs.

67. Find out what makes her insecure.

68. Plan your future together.

69. Do not quarrel over words, but try to find hidden meanings.

70. Practice common courtesies like holding the door for her, pouring her coffee.

71. Ask if you offend her sexually in any way.

72. Ask if she is jealous of anyone.

73. See if she is uncomfortable about the way money is spent.

HE KNEW

74. Take her on dates now and then.
75. Hold her hand in public.
76. Put your arm around her in front of friends.
77. Tell her you love her— often.
78. Remember anniversaries, birthdays, and other special occasions.
79. Learn to enjoy shopping.
80. Teach her to hunt and fish or whatever you enjoy doing.
81. Give her a special gift from time to time.
82. Share the responsibilities around the house.
83. Do not belittle her feminine characteristics.
84. Let her express herself freely, without fear of being called stupid or illogical.
85. Carefully choose your words, especially when angry.
86. Do not criticize her in front of others.
87. Do not let her see you become excited about the physical features of another woman if that bothers her.
88. Be sensitive to other people.
89. Let your family know you want to spend special time with them.
90. Fix dinner for her from time to time.
91. Be sympathetic when she is sick.
92. Call her when you are going to be late.
93. Do not disagree with her in front of the children.
94. Take her out to dinner and for weekend getaways.
95. Do the "little things" she needs from time to time.
96. Give her special time to be alone or with her friends.
97. Buy her what she considers an intimate gift.
98. Read a book she recommends to you.
99. Give her an engraved plaque assuring her of your lasting love.
100. Write her a poem about how special she is.

IF ONLY

If your wife persistently reacts negatively to you, it may be because she perceives a threat to one or both of two important areas: 1) her security 2) her established relationships.

FOR PERSONAL REFLECTION

1. Who did Jesus say would be the greatest in His kingdom? Matthew 20:25–28.
2. If we desire to renew our minds and to think like Christ, we need to consider these:

• What were His thoughts? Philippians 2:5–8.
• What were Paul's thoughts on the same subject? Philippians 2:17, 22, 25.

3. If a husband is to love his wife as Christ loved the church, how does Christ love the church? Ephesians 5:25–27, 29.

3

If Your Wife
Doesn't Win First Place,
You Lose!

"For where your treasure is, there will your heart be also."
Matthew 6:21

Recently I had opportunity to interview some of the married members of a popular cheerleading squad on an NFL football team. I found that they face many of the same problems other married women do. One cheerleader said her greatest disappointment is knowing she is not the most important person in her husband's life.

"Even our dog is more important to him than I am," she said. "He comes home and plays with the dog and then it's more of a when's-dinner-going-to-be-ready? attitude," she sighed.

A woman's sparkling affection toward her husband is diminished when he begins to prefer other activities or people over her. Many times he is not even aware of the way his misplaced priorities damage her and their relationship. For a marriage to flourish, a wife desperately needs to know she has a very special place in her husband's heart. In fact, her husband's relationship with God should be the only priority above his relationship with her.

Many husbands are shocked when their wives leave them "for no reason" after twenty or even thirty years of marriage. They feel they provided everything their wives could have possibly needed—a nice home, a good car, enough money to raise the children. Yet that wasn't enough. Why? A woman needs much more than things.

I have met creative businessmen who make large sums of money with their business skills and who keep their employees satisfied with respect and an awareness of their needs. Isn't it ironic that such intelligent men can go home at night and not even know how to apply the same principles to their wives? Could it be that their most important accomplishments are over at 5:00 P.M.?

Without meaning to, a husband can communicate nonverbally that other people or activities are more important to him than his wife. Haven't you heard of golf widows? Whether it is golf or tennis, club activities or community leadership, your wife and your marital happiness will suffer if most of your time and efforts are directed toward some other interest, with only cold leftovers for her. A wife can feel less important just by comparing the amount of time her husband spends with her to the time he spends elsewhere. Women notice how our eyes light up and our entire personalities change as we become excited about fishing or hunting or other activities. If your wife doesn't sense that same excitement in you when you're with her, she has a gnawing sense of failure because she feels she isn't as attractive to you as are your activities or friends. This can be devastating to a woman's sense of personal worth and security.

My own wife graphically illustrated this very important concept to me during our fifth year of marriage. I arrived home for lunch to find her standing quietly at the kitchen sink, not even interested in talking when I tried to make

OFFICE WIDOW, TV WIDOW

MAGAZINE WIDOW

conversation. In a moment of insight, I perceived that I was in hot water. I remembered her coolness toward me during the previous few days, which I had mistakenly attributed to some sort of "hormonal change."

"Is there anything wrong between us?" I asked her.

"It doesn't matter. You wouldn't understand anyway," she answered.

"Funny thing, I'm losing my desire to go back to work right now. I can see there are some real problems here. Wouldn't you like to talk about it? I'm not sure what I'm doing wrong."

"Even if I told you, either you wouldn't understand or you wouldn't change, so what's the use? Let's don't talk about it. It's too painful. It discourages me and disappoints me when you say you're going to do something and then you don't."

HAVEN'T I HEARD THAT

But I gently resisted, telling her that I wished she would share it with me, that I just didn't understand. Finally, she was able to verbalize what actions during the past five years had driven a wedge between us and were causing me to violate an important biblical principle.

"You'd really rather be at work, or with your friends, or counseling people than spending time with me," she said.

I asked her to explain.

"If someone calls you when we have plans, you're liable to say, 'Let me check with my wife and see if I can't postpone our plans.' I just can't believe you would do that to me over and over again."

I explained how it was easier for me to turn her down than to say no to other people.

"What about when I cook a special dinner, sometimes even with candlelight? You'll come home or call and say you've had to make other plans. You go off somewhere with other people as if I didn't even exist, as if it didn't even mean anything that I've gone to extra-special effort for you."

She continued, "I don't care any more. I don't even want to do these special things for you. I've been disappointed so many times that I just can't handle it emotionally."

She made me realize that although I always had time for someone in need of counseling, I made little effort to spend meaningful time with her. When I did spend time with her, she said, I didn't have the same concentration or excitement about being with her.

I listened as she revealed her innermost feelings for several hours. I really didn't know what to do, and I wasn't sure I'd be able to change. But I could understand her complaints. I had neglected her and offended her with my unloving ways. However, when I agreed with her, she was unresponsive, and I could tell she was no longer expecting anything from our relationship.

She helped me discover that I was ignoring the biblical principle found in 1 Peter 3:7, and since then I've come to realize that it's the cornerstone of all relationships! *Grant her honor.* Honor basically means to attach high value, worth, or importance to a person or thing. Norma felt less important than my vocation and activities. Without realizing it, I was not honoring her as the most important person in my life, second only to my relationship with Christ.

"Could you forgive me for the way I've treated you?" I asked. "I'm willing to change. I'll really plan on changing."

"Sure, I've heard that song before," she said skeptically.

I didn't know how long it would take for me to reform. But I knew the next time someone called right before dinner I would have to ask, "Is this an emergency, or can we work it out tomorrow?" I had to show her I really meant business about valuing her and meeting her needs *first.*

HE KNEW

I *wanted* to tell her she was the most important person in my life. I really *wanted* to feel that way. At first I didn't have those feelings, but I *wanted* to have them. As I tried to make her more important to me than anyone else, I soon began to *feel* she was top priority. Feelings *follow* thoughts and actions. In other words, the warm inner feeling I have for Norma began to burn *after* I placed the "queen's crown" upon her head. (I shouldn't have been surprised because in Matthew 6 we're told that what we "treasure" or "value" is what we'll have feelings for.)

My pride was broken, my ego bruised, and my feelings wounded in numerous falls from marital harmony during the first two years of living these principles. Because I tried so hard to make it work, Norma finally believed I was earnest in my endeavor to change. But it took two years to convince her—and it may take you that long to convince your wife.

I learned from Norma and other wives that women need to see effort and not hear mere promises. Give your wife time to watch you climb the mountain if she doesn't believe what you say initially. Show her you are learning to scale the cliffs and hurdle the crevices. The more *consistently* loving we are as husbands, the more trustworthy we become to our wives. Soon they will join us as we climb hand-over-hand toward the goal of a loving marriage.

The most important way I've ever expressed my love to Norma was when I finally attached a high value to her, when I decided that next to my relationship with God and His Word, she is worth more to me than anything on this earth—and she knows it.

41

THE EVIDENCE WIVES NEED BEFORE THEY WILL BELIEVE THEIR HUSBANDS

Wives need proof of change over a consistent period of time in at least three areas before they will believe their husbands' commitment.

Careful Listening Without Justification or Argument *HA!*

Can you imagine a husband being able to justify everything he ever did to hurt his wife? Wayne thought he could. He and his wife couldn't talk for more than fifteen minutes before falling into a heated argument. Inevitably, through his logical deductions, the argument ended up being her fault.

Finally, Wayne told Cathy he really wanted to change, and to love her. A few hours later she suggested a quiet little vacation, just for the two of them to get reacquainted. "Couldn't we just take a week's vacation?" she asked.

"Are you kidding?" he replied, crushing her hopes for better understanding. "You mean you want me to pay rent here at the apartment and then pay for a motel too? That's double rent!"

The topic developed into a fight that led to more fights as the months went by, until their relationship deteriorated and she finally left. He had refused to listen to her needs without arguing and lost her as a result. Tragically, even today, several years later, he still doesn't understand what ended their relationship.

It is often difficult for a man to converse with his wife without challenging the meaning of various words she uses to explain how she feels inside. If a husband can *overlook the actual words* his wife uses to express herself and instead actively pursue *what she means*, fewer arguments will take place. One man I know finds it almost impossible to do this. When his wife uses phrases like "You *never* do this," or "You *always* do that," he will inevitably say, "Now, dear, I don't *always* do that," or "Did I do it yesterday?" Or he begins to analyze her statement to prove its fallacy. In ten minutes, they're off on another hot discussion. It is essential in communication to *look past the surface words* to the real meaning behind the words.

There is no meaning in a word. Meaning is in people.

Everyone has his or her own definition for a given word. We attach meanings to words based on our own unique experiences. So when we attempt to communicate with another person, we use words we believe will accurately convey our thoughts. For instance, in this book I may use words that you enjoy or words that irritate you. You might even be indifferent to my words because you have another frame of reference or because my definitions might be different from yours. That is why I try to illustrate all the important points I make, probing for our common point of reference.

If we can stop justifying our actions and quit arguing about the words our wives use, we can get down to the heart of the matter. We can try rephrasing our wives' statements until they say we have grasped their meaning. "Is this what you're saying, dear?" or "Is this what I'm hearing?" At all cost, avoid sarcastic questions like, "Is this what you're having trouble saying?" A budding relationship between husband and wife can be stunted by an attitude of male superiority. YOUR'RE KIDDING

Quickness to Admit Error

Countless wives and children have told me how their family relationships were weakened because of a husband's or father's unwillingness to admit his errors. Though husbands sometimes think admission of error reveals their weaknesses, the opposite is true. Just think back through your own life to the times when someone admitted his or her offense to you. Chances are, your respect for him or her increased, not decreased.

A friend of mine told me about the time he made a racially derogatory statement to an associate during the day. The man was offended; however, the situation was not discussed. My friend drove away feeling somewhat uneasy and guilty for what he had said. Before he reached home, he turned around and drove back to confront the man.

Walking into the room, he said, "A few minutes ago I said something very offensive to you. I know it was wrong, and I have come back to ask if you could forgive me for what I said."

The man nearly fell over. Of course he forgave him, and I'm sure his respect for my friend doubled. A humble admission of wrong produces positive results. When a husband admits he has hurt his wife, she feels better just knowing he understands. His admission of wrong can produce a much stronger marriage. Not only that, it demonstrates that he is a wise man because the Scriptures tell us only the wise seek correction.

Patience When She Is Reluctant to Believe He's Changed

What if you've been doing everything within your power to let your wife know she has first place in your life, and she still doesn't believe you've changed? Do you throw up your arms in disgust? Or do you gently persuade her over a period of time? I hope you choose the latter. Her initial respect for you wasn't lost overnight, and it can't be regained in a day. Show her that no matter how long it takes, you want to earn her respect.

TWO REASONS WHY A WIFE CAN BECOME LESS IMPORTANT TO HER HUSBAND

What causes a man to come home after work, pick up his young son, and kiss and cuddle him without even greeting his wife? How can a husband walk straight to the garage to begin a project without even acknowledging his arrival to his wife as he passes by her in the kitchen? Why does a man *lose* affection and enthusiasm for his wife after marriage? I think there are two major reasons.

1. A man will pursue and charm a woman with words or flowers or whatever he needs to do to *win her.* But after the wedding, he feels he has conquered her. She is his, so he doesn't have to maintain the same level of enthusiasm and creativity as he did before they married. She is his emotionally and legally. The husband may say to himself, "I have my wife. Now I need to conquer my business . . . become a better hunter . . . begin a family. . . ." Each frontier is viewed as a new conquest, a new experience.

2. Almost anything is sweet to a starving man, but when he's full, even honey nauseates him (Prov. 27:7). In a very real sense, a man is filled up when he marries because his wife is now a part of him. He believes he has experienced knowing her in every way—spiritually, emotionally, mentally, and physically. He may feel there is nothing left to know about her. He is satisfied and, therefore, has a tendency to look for other potential "frontiers."

HOW TO GAIN YOUR WIFE'S LOVE AND MORE

If it came down to an evening with your friends or a night with your wife, she needs to know you would choose her company just because you enjoy being with her. In the same way, if it came to the children or her, she needs to know she would be your choice. She needs to know she's Number One. When she is satisfied that she's in first place in your life, she will encourage you to do the other things you like doing. For example, I am taking six weeks away from my wife and children to write this book. Several years ago my wife would have been crushed at the mere suggestion of such a long separation. Yet today she is as enthusiastic about it as I am because she knows I will be able to fulfill *our* dream of writing our inner convictions about marriage. More importantly, she knows I would rather be with her than with my typewriter and editor.

Putting your wife in the Number One slot just below God doesn't shackle you to the house; instead, it frees you of the dread of going home.

"Why don't you let me go the meeting alone tonight so you can go to the basketball game?" Mary said. Her husband was pleasantly shocked. Not so long ago they had had misunderstandings about his insatiable appetite for basketball. In fact, they were thinking about separating because he did not have the knowledge or skills he needed to treat Mary right, and she did not have the emotional strength to continue living with him or loving him. Today he regularly puts her before his work, his activities, etc. And Mary is now free to encourage his outside interests, knowing she's at the top of his list.

My wife also encourages me to enjoy my interests in hunting and fishing because she feels secure in her position of importance. If an emergency arose, she knows my first commitment would be to taking care of her or the children, not to my recreational enjoyment.

> The more important a woman feels she is to her husband, the more she encourages him to do the activities she knows he enjoys.

Do you wonder whether your wife feels she is more important to you than other people or things in your life? Complete the following exercise, and I think you will find out.

First, list your favorite spare-time activities.

_____

_____

_____

_____

_____

What is an enjoyable after-work activity for you?

Monday _____

Tuesday _____

Wednesday _____

Thursday _____

Friday _____

Saturday _____

Sunday _____

Where do you enjoy taking your vacations?

_____

_____

_____

Now, look back over these three lists and ask yourself, *"Is there anything on the lists I would rather do than be with my wife?"* Probably so. And if so, chances are you have already "communicated" to your wife that she is not as important to you as your activities, even though you have never uttered those words. Since a woman has tremendous perception, she knows where your heart is, even when you haven't said a word. But that doesn't mean it's too late to adjust your priorities.

YOUR WIFE'S "RADAR" CAN DETECT YOUR SINCERITY

What a man values, he takes good care of. Or as Christ said, "Where your treasure is, there will your heart be also" (Matt. 6:21). If your hobby is fishing, you probably hesitate to loan out your best rod and reel. If you enjoy hunting, you probably know how to carefully oil and polish guns. Based on the amount of time you spend on each activity, your wife can sense which is most important to you. If she doesn't feel that you are as careful with her as you are with your other interests, she will know she is not as important. That feeling shatters her self-worth and can result in physical as well as emotional problems. The emotions she struggles with now may surface years later in the form of serious and expensive physical problems.

However, some husbands feel threatened by the thought of giving their wives special treatment, fearing they will lose out with their friends, career, or hobbies. They falsely believe if they give up other activities for the sake of being with their wives, they will give them up forever. Remember, when a wife feels she is the most important, she gets excited about her husband being able to do the things he wants to do. But don't try and deceive her! Simply telling her she's first so she'll let you out to do what you want doesn't work. In fact, if she finds out you've tried to manipulate her, you may be faced with major problems concerning her trust in you and her own feelings of worth.

HOW I GAINED MY WIFE'S LOVE AND EVERYTHING ELSE

After ten years of marriage, I felt I was finally becoming a success at my work. I was privileged to speak regularly for various organizations in our city and throughout the country. My wife and I had a beautiful home and two children. What more could a man want? Then from my point of view, a tragedy occurred in my marriage. Norma became pregnant with our third child. I was not enthusiastic. If anything, I was depressed, realizing our youngest had only been out of diapers for two years. I was just starting to enjoy my children, and the thought of another little baby around the house was almost overwhelming, particularly when the doctor had told us specifically that we couldn't have any more children.

Although I tried to be nice to Norma, I couldn't hide my disappointment. I was afraid I might not be able to travel as much and would be forced to take a less prestigious position in the company. My work load increased as the months passed, and I warned my wife I would not be able to help her with the children because of job demands. Even on the day our son was born, I worried about the added hardships he would add to my vocational dreams.

Norma's health suffered during the first year after our son's birth because of the long night hours and the responsibility of taking care of two other small children. Our baby had to have surgery and was often sick, adding to her burden. How insensitive I was during that year! Whenever the baby would cry at night or need special attention, I would quickly remind Norma he was her child. She had wanted another baby, not I.

A year passed in this way before Norma finally said to me, "I can't take it any more. I wish I had the emotional and physical strength to take care of the kids, discipline and train them, but I just can't do it with an absentee father."

She wasn't demanding. She wasn't angry. She was simply stating the facts. She had had it. I could see the *urgency* and *calmness* in her facial expressions and realized that she desperately needed my help. I faced a major decision. Should I go to my boss and ask for a different job in the company? Ask for a job that would allow me more time at home? It was a struggle because I knew I could get a less prestigious and less lucrative job. I felt I would have to sacrifice some of my career goals. Inwardly, I felt resentment toward my son and my wife for being weak. But I gave in.

In nervousness and embarrassment, I approached my boss to explain I needed more time at home because of the children. "Is there any possibility that I could have a different job that would allow me to stay home more?"

My boss graciously cooperated by giving me another job. But to me the new job was a demotion. I was asked to do some things that only a few weeks earlier I had been training my subordinates to do. What a blow, which did nothing but fuel my resentment!

I was devastated for a while, but soon I became interested in home life. I actually looked forward to five o'clock. My family and I began doing more things together, like camping and other special activities. Before long, a deeper love blossomed within both Norma and me. Norma began to feel more physically alert which, in turn, made her more cheerful and outgoing. She changed some habits I disliked without any pressure from me. My "big" career sacrifice seemed smaller every day in comparison to the richer relationship we were developing.

Within a few months, my boss gave me a new position in the company that I liked much better than the one I had given up. By this time, Norma was so secure with me that she had no resentment toward my new job or any necessary travel that went with it. I gave in and gave up at first, but I won in the long run. That's almost exactly how Christ explains the principle of exchange in Mark 8:34–37.

Even to this day, if I ask our son Michael, "Why are you so important to Dad?" he'll say, "Because I brought you back to Mama and the family."

THE INCREDIBLE RESULTS OF MAKING YOUR WIFE FEEL IMPORTANT

One morning Sandy was so sexually responsive to Rick that he was stunned and surprised by her excitement. How did Rick motivate her? With one very simple statement. He was getting ready for work that morning, running a little late, when he heard Sandy complaining of a growing headache and neckache.

"Let me rub your neck," he offered.

"No, you don't have time," she replied. "You've got to get to work."

His usual response would have been, "Yeah, you're right. I don't want to be late. But I hope you feel better. Take an aspirin."

On this particular morning he said, "I tell you what. I'd rather be with you any day. Let me rub your neck." As he gently massaged her tense muscles, he continued, *"Work can wait . . . you're more important to me."* She was so thrilled with his attitude and so encouraged by his sensitivity and gentleness that she said she could hardly resist giving herself to him in every way.

We men are not aware of the effect we have on our wives by being gentle and tender, showing our unshakable devotion.

Do you want a more enjoyable marriage? It's possible. And it all starts by loving your wife more than any person or any activity.

Here are a few questions you can ask your wife to open up a discussion concerning her real feelings about the place she shares in your life:

HE KNEW

1. Do you feel you are the most important person in my life?
2. Are there any activities in my life you feel are more important to me than you are?
3. Are there any special ways you believe I could better communicate how important you are to me?

Remember, the more you do to build a valuable, healthy relationship, the better you'll feel about your marriage. If you change any of your activities because you want to enrich your relationship, at first you may feel you're giving up your

---

How a military officer loved his wife out of a mental hospital.

The psychiatrist had prescribed that his wife be admitted to the local mental hospital. He was stunned and challenged, but had no idea how to help her. He sought counsel from the chaplain and learned he should allow his wife to sit in his lap and share her true feelings about him.

He followed this advice with great difficulty because it hurt to hear the things she said he was doing to weaken their marriage. As she was talking, the telephone rang, and he felt "saved by the bell." She was angry because she thought he would probably not return. But she overheard one statement he made that not only kept her from a breakdown but prompted her to slip into a nightgown and actually desire to arouse him (something she had not done in years). After the call, she calmly snuggled back into his lap.

What had he said to his commanding officer?

He simply said, "Sir, could someone else take that assignment tonight? I'm in the middle of a very important time with my wife. It's serious, and I really don't want to leave at this point." That military officer had begun to prove to his wife that she was of high value to him. As a result, her mental condition stabilized, and she never had to go to the hospital.

---

favorite pastime. But in the long run, you'll not only gain a better marriage, but a greater freedom to enjoy other areas of life. Today I wouldn't trade my deep friendship with Norma for anything on this earth. I am finding that the more important a man's wife is to him, the more she encourages him to enjoy life.

FOR PERSONAL REFLECTION

1. What is the basic meaning of the word "honor"? 1 Peter 3:7.
2. How can your emotional feelings for your mate grow? Matthew 6:21.

4

**Your Wife Needs
Your Shoulder,
Not Your Mouth**

"Put on a heart of compassion, kindness, humility, gentleness and patience."

Colossians 3:12

As I pulled into the driveway, I heard a sickening thump
under the tire. Only a few seconds earlier our cat had been
running expectantly toward our car to welcome us home.

"Watch out for Puff," Norma said.

"Oh, he'll get out of the way," I replied.

I hadn't been driving fast. *How fast can you pull into a
driveway?* I thought.

"Oh, no!" I whispered. "Can someone get me out of this
mess?" My family thought it was just another one of my
jokes about wanting to get rid of our two cats.

Our oldest son jumped out of the car, looked underneath,
and fell to the ground screaming. Our daughter began sobbing, and our youngest son woke up from his nap to join the
chorus. Bedlam set in. They all started accusing me of
purposely killing the cat. In fact, I was accused of things
that would have put me in jail for years. How I regretted
the times I had joked about it.

Puff was the kitten of our other cat. We all loved the

mother cat, but they loved Puff much more. We had kept the kitten because of his "puffy" hernia. His stomach grew larger and larger until finally I had to give in and take him to a veterinarian to have the hernia repaired. But the operation was a failure. A few months later I had to take him back for another operation. And I didn't even want the cat in the first place! I told my family, "This cat sure is costing me a lot." I was saying things some men typically say, blind to the hurt I was causing my family.

Now that I had run over the cat, I was under attack. When they started screaming at me, I wanted to yell back. But the things Norma had shared with me in the past about herself and our children strangled the words. "Don't talk. Just hold me or hold the kids whenever there's a tragedy," she had said.

They were making so much racket in the front yard that I knew the neighbors were going to think I was killing them. I was so embarrassed and crushed that I herded them all into the house. Then I put my arm around Kari and hugged her. But as I hugged Greg, I could tell he didn't want me to touch him. I tried to put my arm around Norma, but she gave me one of those familiar looks a woman saves for times when her husband bombs out.

"This is what you always wanted, isn't it?" she asked. "You wanted him dead." With that, she marched into the bedroom and closed the door.

But I still didn't say anything. I didn't get angry, although I felt my family misunderstood me. I knew that raising my voice wouldn't help. Since Michael didn't want me to touch him either, Greg and I went out to the driveway to get Puff and bury him. We took him to our little burial ground where Peter, our rabbit, rests. Greg was still sobbing, "Dad, life will never be the same." Greg loved that cat just about as much as you can love anything. As Greg and I buried him, I prayed, and Greg concluded the funeral service.

I felt nauseous as I went back inside. There stood twelve-year-old Kari comforting five-year-old Michael. "Michael, it was Puff's time to go. It was Puff's time."

When Greg was getting ready for bed, I went to his room and held him. His eyes red, he asked, "Dad, what am I going to do when I come home from school? What am I going to do, dad? Puff won't be there to jump into my arms." And like Greg, I had tears streaming down my cheeks.

Courageous little Kari was standing in the hall after putting Michael to bed. "Well, Dad, it's all over," she said. "It was Puff's time. I tell you what, Dad, I think we can eat those donuts now." (We had bought donuts and milk after church, planning a quiet family snack.)

"Kari, you can if you want, but I just wouldn't be able to eat. I just can't eat tonight," I told her.

Opening the door to our bedroom, I wondered if my wife was ready to face me yet. She had told me many times in the past, "Don't demand anything. Wait until I am able to respond to you."

I got down on my knees next to her, gently touching her hand, and asked, "How are you feeling?"

"I'm feeling better. I know you didn't mean to murder Puff," she said.

I could have reacted to her statement in anger but I only said, "That's okay. I understand. You know all those things I said when I was joking about Puff? I really feel bad about them. You can rest assured I'll never joke about things like that again. Would it make you feel better if we made Angel an 'inside' cat from now on?"

From time to time for a few weeks, I would say to Norma, "You know, I really do feel bad that you don't have Puff around to jump up into your arms." She would put her head down on my shoulder and say, "Yeah, I know, I feel bad too." Through that painful experience, I learned more about comforting my wife than I could have in years of troublefree existence.

Let your wife teach you how you can best meet her needs during a crisis or when she's discouraged and losing energy.

Probably the most important lesson my wife taught me on how to comfort her was when she told me in a calm way that she could not handle my busy work schedule along with the pressures of the children and the home. *By coming to me without threats to explain her limitations*, she touched something within me. I was eager to comfort her. I don't know if she stirred my protective manly feelings or what, but when she told me she couldn't take the pressure I was putting on her and that she might be close to a collapse, I was motivated to relieve her of that pressure.

I have found that this nonthreatening approach works even in a father-daughter relationship. A university graduate student came to me because of a poor relationship with her father. Financially, he had been very generous to her, but she needed his love and gentleness much more than she needed his money. I tried to work with her father, explaining what I had learned about women. "Comfort her," I suggested. "Be tender and gentle. Don't lecture her." But he couldn't grasp it, although he is a very skillful and intelligent lawyer, quite successful in his profession. (I have noticed that my lawyer friends have a difficult time being tender and loving without lecturing. They have been inculcated with the need for logical expression.)

"I tried to take my life last week," this young woman told me. "I just cannot handle the emotional pressure I'm under with my father."

"You've got choices," I said.

"What?"

"You can respond to your father in a way that you and I know will bring healing to your life."

"I'm not able to do that," she said wearily.

"Okay, then you can call your father and say to him, 'Daddy, I love you. I wish that I could spend more time with you, but, Daddy, I feel like I just can't handle seeing you right now. I can't emotionally handle the way you treat me—your lectures, your insensitivity, and your harshness. As much as I wish I could, as much as I wish I were stronger, I just can't handle it right now!'"

This girl has unique needs and qualities. Nobody could tell her she needed to be stronger. She is who she is. To tell her to be what she can't be is like saying to the sun, "Don't come up tomorrow." It's reality!

Happily, her father was motivated to change, thinking, *I must really be insensitive. My own daughter can't handle my presence. She can't even handle a phone call from me.*

Many men don't realize that tender love through a gentle touch and listening ear is all a woman needs at times—just a comforting hug, a loving statement like, "I understand. You're hurting, aren't you? You're feeling under a lot of pressure, aren't you?" Listening to her talk without making critical comments or offering quick solutions is important.

GIVE HER YOUR SHOULDER, NOT YOUR MOUTH

Your goal should be to become a gentle, loving, and tender husband who does not lecture. Lectures during stressful times only create more stress. This was a new concept to me because I wasn't fortunate enough to have a father who knew how to be tender to his wife. I wasn't aware of my wife's needs for tenderness until a few years ago. No one had ever told me that one of a woman's greatest needs is tenderness and a husband who will listen instead of lecture, and even if someone had, I don't think I would have understood. (I should have been able to figure it out, though, because when I am down, I like people to be gentle and comforting to me.)

I'll never forget what one woman told me: "If my husband would only put his arms around me and hold me, without lecturing me, when I am feeling blue!" But Lecture #734 would begin as he told her she would feel better if she took an aspirin . . . if she were more organized . . . if she wouldn't wear herself down so much . . . if she would discipline the children better. . . .

"Have you ever told him what you need?" I asked.

"Are you kidding? I'd be embarrassed," she laughed. "Come on, you're kidding."

"No. He probably doesn't know what to do. He doesn't know you need to be held instead of lectured. Why don't you tell him during a calm conversation some day?"

"That does kind of make sense to me. A lot of times when I am down and crying and all upset, he'll ask, 'What do you want me to do?' I just flare up and say, 'If I have to tell you what to do, it would wreck the whole idea.'"

As a husband, I recommend that you ask your wife when and how you need to hold her when she needs to be comforted. Ask her what circumstances prompt her to seek your gentle caring arms and touch. You can't dream them up on your own. We just can't perceive the deep feelings of other people. We've got to draw them out and then *practice*,

practice, practice the skills of meeting our wives' needs.

The first time I ever tried to ski, I rode a rope pulley to the top of a small hill. The hill looked a lot bigger from the top than it did from the bottom.

I thought, *No way am I gonna go down this hill.* So I sat down on the back of my skis and scooted all the way down.

Even if you have to scoot instead of ski your way through the skills in this chapter at first, remember that you'll eventually be able to get to your feet. This book is certainly not an exhaustive marriage manual, but it is a start. Believe me, if you practice what is written here, you and your wife can have a more loving marriage.

When I was first learning the art of comforting my wife, we had an experience that took every ounce of self-control I could muster. But I came through a stronger man, encouraged by my new-found strength. I want you to imagine yourself in my situation. How would you have reacted?

I had bought a dumpy-looking boat for $400 because we wanted to do more things together as a family. That same night my son and I decided to take it for a quick trip to the lake, only five minutes from our house, just to see how it ran. Because of my inexperience as a boater, the wind blew the boat back to the bank the first time I put it in. I got wet and frustrated trying to push it out again. After an irritating ten minutes trying to start the cantankerous thing, the boat wouldn't go faster than ten miles an hour. Something was obviously wrong. I was quite a way from the shore before I realized I had better get back in case the motor stalled.

Then—"Dad, the boat's sinking!" Greg cried. I looked behind me and saw the foot of water that had gurgled in. The previous owner had taken the plug out the last time it had rained but had forgotten to tell me. With the hull full of water, I couldn't find the hole for the plug. Luckily we didn't sink. I put the boat back on the trailer, determined to take it back first thing in the morning. I was a little embarrassed to have the dumpy-looking thing parked in front of my house anyway.

A boat dealer told me it would take $150 to fix the engine's broken seal, so I returned it to the owner who had promised me I could have my money back if I didn't like it.

When I left home early that morning, I had agreed to be back by eleven o'clock so Norma could go shopping. Retrieving my money took longer than I had planned, and I arrived home an hour-and-a-half late. In the meantime, Norma had decided to take our minimotor home to the grocery store. Trying to turn it around in the driveway, she accidentally drove too close to the house and sheared off a section of the roof. As the roof fell, it put a huge dent in the front of the motor home.

When I pulled into the driveway at 12:30, I saw part of the roof lying in the driveway next to the dented motor home. I just laughed out loud, more out of desperation than humor.

I wanted to say to my wife, "Oh, no, $500 at least to fix this. Where did you get your driver's license, at a garage sale?" I wanted to lecture her angrily and then ignore her for a while.

For once, I remembered what I was supposed to do. I told myself, "Keep your mouth shut and put your arms around her. Just hold her. Don't say anything, okay?"

However, my basic human nature told me, "Give her a lecture. Let your anger out. Express it."

My mind finally triumphed over my will. I put my arms around her and said gently, "You must feel terrible, don't you?" even though war was still raging inside me. We went into the house and sat on the couch. I let her talk her feelings out.

I held her, and after a couple of minutes I felt good because I could feel the tenderness begin to flow from me. Soon I was fine, and she was encouraged. Minutes later, a carpenter friend drove up who had already heard about the accident. We had the roof patched and painted in two hours.

It felt good not to be angry for once. I hadn't offended my wife, shouted at the kids, or diminished any of the beauty of our relationship. I could have reverted to my old excuse, "Well, I just can't keep from blowing up." Instead, I had one of those encouraging victories.

My new-found sensitivity has been tested on several occasions. Once I almost blew it on a fishing trip. I normally become completely oblivious to my family and the world when I'm near a stream, totally "submerging" myself in the exhilarating environment of fishing: the smell of the air, the tension when a fish strikes, the sound of the stream. . . . Oops! Back to the story.

When we pulled up in our minimotor home beside a beautiful stream, my heart was pounding. I could hardly wait to get my reel rigged up. First, I rigged the kids' reels and told them, "Look, if you get tangled up, you're on your own." (I used to get so frustrated when I was trying to fish and they were yelling, "Dad, I can't get this reeled in." I wanted to devote my entire energy to fishing on my own.)

I found the perfect spot: a nice deep hole in a pool in front of a big boulder. I threw in the lure and let it wander naturally to the bottom of the pool. It swirled around and WHAM! I got my first trout! I had nearly caught the limit when Greg came running up. I was sure he was about to jump into the stream and spook the fish. I was already upset and angry from his interruption when he said, "Dad! Kari broke her leg!"

Kari broke her leg? What a time to break her leg! I couldn't believe she would do this to me. It was hard for me to leave, but I gave the line to Greg and said, "Don't break it. Don't get it tangled up. Just keep it in there." I ran in Kari's direction, avoiding the big pool. After all, I didn't want to scare the fish.

Downstream, Kari was crying. "Daddy, I think I broke my leg."

When I looked at it, I realized it was only bruised.

"Don't touch it," I said. "It's not broken, it's just bruised. Put your leg in this cold water to soak for a few minutes."

I'm really embarrassed to tell the rest of the story, but maybe you can learn from my insensitivity. I ran back to the fishing hole and caught a few more trout before walking back to where Kari was crying. "Dad, this water is cold."

I rather roughly got her up to walk, but she couldn't. When I tried to hoist her up on the bank and couldn't, she started crying again and said, "Dad, you're so rough with me. Can't you be *tender*?" Something flashed when she said that word. It reminded me of all the times my wife and other women have told me, "What we need is tenderness and gentleness, not harshness. We don't need lectures." And I couldn't even be tender with my eleven-year-old daughter. I had already lectured Kari because I felt she was interrupting my day. "Why didn't you look first?" I had asked her.

Just who was more important anyway? Those trout or my precious daughter? It was hard for me to face, but those trout had been more important to me. I had let fishing and my own desires endanger my only daughter. I was wrong, and I should have known better!

When I came to my senses, I hung my head low and said, "Kari, I've been so wrong to be harsh with you. I really feel bad. Would you forgive me?"

"Yeah, I'll forgive you, Dad."

"Kari, you are more important to me than any fish, and I want you to know that. I was so carried away by this activity today that I really hurt you, didn't I?"

We just held each other for a while, and then she looked up into my eyes and asked gently, "Dad, did you use deodorant today?"

HELPING YOUR WIFE OVERCOME DEPRESSION

Both men and women experience stress daily. Some days are worse than others—like the day I ran over Puff. Psychologists tell us that stressful experiences and prolonged anger affect our mind, our emotions, and our body. The amount of stress we experience in each of these areas can mean the difference between happiness or depression. Positive input in any *one* area has been proven to have beneficial effects on all the other areas. If a husband is tender with his wife, for example, he lifts her emotions and, in turn, helps her in other dimensions of her life.

According to Dr. Jerry Day, a clinical psychologist from Tucson, Arizona, if a wife has at least four of the following symptoms she could be diagnosed as depressed. As a husband, you need to know these signs in order to be able to comfort your wife more effectively. Let's not forget that a major destroyer of any relationship is hurt and anger held inside.

General Symptoms of Depression

1. Sadness
2. Hopelessness
3. Loss of humor
4. Premature awakening
5. Early morning awakening
6. Insomnia
7. Feeling better as the day wears on
8. Loss of sexual interest
9. Loss of appetite and weight
10. Sharp increase of appetite and weight gain
11. Vague physical complaints
12. Sense of personal loss (death of a close relative, loss of job, etc.)
13. Poor concentration and memory
14. Deep sighing or moaning

Should you detect these symptoms in your wife, you should comfort her first with statements like, "Honey, I'm not sure I know how you feel, but I really want to. And I want to help you work through whatever it is that is discouraging you." Then use the information below as a guideline to *help her* out of depression. Remember, if your wife is depressed, it may or may not be something you've contributed to—but it is always your responsibility to help.

1. If your wife has at least four of the above symptoms, encourage her to have a complete physical examination. Her symptoms might be caused by a hormone or vitamin deficiency or by a physical illness.

2. Avoid lecturing her. Arguing with her only makes her feel you don't understand. But sending her a card or flowers can lift her emotionally. Help your children do something special for her. For example, you can go down to the store and buy a small roll of shelf paper. Roll it out and on it paste magazine pictures that depict things you appreciate about her. With brightly colored pens, write affectionate words all over the banner. Roll it up with a pretty bow and present it to her as a family. Your thoughtful gesture will affect her emotions and *help* lift her out of the darkness.

3. Listen to your wife with the "third ear." In other words, listen for her emotional message. What is she trying to say?

Can you understand the meaning behind her words? Try saying something like, "I don't know why this terrible thing has happened to you, but I can really see that it has deeply upset you." By saying those words, you will allow her time to gain physical strength through your understanding.

4. Help her feel better by "blocking" her symptoms. Dr. Day explained this concept to me as follows: Whenever actors are on stage, they have to overdo and exaggerate to communicate a thought to the audience. Though they feel they are exaggerating, the audience perceives their behavior as normal. Dr. Day believes it is important for you to exaggerate your wife's problem so she will really believe you understand how badly she feels. She will receive your statements as normal, though you may feel you have overdone it.

For example, suggest a very hard project for her. It can be something physically exhausting like jogging, or something else that requires fierce mental effort. Tell her, "Maybe you ought to do something serious to get over this." Many times this shocks a depressed person into reality. They come away feeling, "Things aren't that bad."

When things seem hopeless, though, a depressed person often feels like sleeping the day away. Nothing could be worse. Help your wife get up and go out, even if you have to go shopping with her. My wife sometimes feels like hiding under the blanket when she's down or feeling blue, even though she knows she will feel better if she gets up and goes to an exercise class or becomes vigorously involved in an activity.

5. Another helpful therapy for depression is writing down our thoughts. A certain "washing of the soul" occurs when we record our thoughts while in depression, Dr. Day says. Buy your wife a notebook and encourage her to write down the ways you or others have hurt her.

Better yet, encourage her to write down the benefits that will enter her life as a result of the depressing things that have happened to her. She may resist at first, saying she can't think of a single benefit. You may need to come up with at least one benefit for her before she can get started. The more benefits she uncovers, the better she will feel. Most women who do this exercise end up telling me, "Things really aren't so bad." In fact, this is so important that I've written an entire book to help people find value in troubled times. *Joy That Lasts* can assist you in helping your wife actually find benefit in trials and gain a whole new perspective on anger, worry, fear, hurt feelings, and guilt.

Even when your wife can't take time to write down her feelings, you can help her avoid negative thinking. Gently steer her away from the two words, "If only." Those words, one psychiatrist said, have kept more people in depression than any others. "If only I hadn't . . . if only I would . . . if only he had. . . ." Those two words can tear up a person emotionally, mentally, and physically.

6. During stressful times, encourage your wife to relax her muscles. I practice regularly an exercise recommended by Dr. Day. I can personally testify that this ten-minute relaxing technique has, at times, made me feel like I've just had four hours of deep sleep. It renews creativity and strength.

Allow your body's natural relaxing mechanism to work: relax in a chair or on a bed, take several deep breaths, tighten every muscle in your body for as long as you can hold one deep breath, and then exhale. Visualize your muscles relaxing, and then don't move a muscle for the remainder of the ten minutes.

7. Gain a firm commitment from your wife to begin and continue a vigorous physical exercise program. Norma has

joined a women's health club just to have a place to exercise when she feels discouraged. Physical exercise helps a person mentally and emotionally. Those who work with depressed people say it is one of the most important areas of therapy.

8. Part of being wise is discerning when we need help as well. If your wife gets and stays depressed for longer than three weeks, you need to think seriously about calling your pastor or a Christian counselor to help you make a difference in your loved one's life.

How Does Your Wife Need to Be Comforted?

Why not ask her to help you understand how and when she needs comfort? Encourage her to be patient with you until you master the skill of tenderly comforting her.

FOR PERSONAL REFLECTION

1. Is it natural to be comforting and gentle during tension or a crisis? Colossians 3:8–14; 4:6.
2. Do you understand your wife's needs during a crisis? 1 Peter 3:7. Write out her response to this question, too.

5

Climbing Out
Of Marriage's
Deepest Pit

> "It is inevitable that stumbling blocks should come, but
> woe to him through whom they come!"
>
> Luke 17:1

It was 4:00 P.M. on Valentine's Day when I remembered
my basketball game. I reached for the phone to call Norma,
my bride of less than a year.

"Honey, I forgot to tell you I have a basketball game
tonight. We're supposed to be there about 7:00. I'll pick
you up about 6:30."

Silence hung heavily on the line before she answered,
"But this is Valentine's Day."

"Yeah, I know, but I need to be there tonight because
I promised the team. I don't want to let them down."

"But I have a special dinner prepared with candles
and—"

"Can you hold it off until tomorrow?" She didn't answer,
so I continued. (What I was about to say caused a great
deal of damage in our relationship. Like many young husbands, I didn't have the slightest hint of how deeply this
would wound her.) "Honey, you know how important it is
for a wife to submit to her husband. I really need to be

71

there tonight, and if we're going to start off with good habits in the early part of our marriage, now is the time to begin. If I'm going to be the leader of this family, I need to make the decision."

"Ice" perfectly describes the reception I received when I picked her up. It was easy to see I had severely offended her, but I figured she had to learn to be submissive sometime, and we might as well start now.

The lifeless expression on her face grew worse as the evening wore on. When we returned home after the game, I noticed that the table was all set up for a special dinner—candles, our best dishes, and pretty napkins. She still wasn't speaking to me the next day, so I rushed to the florist to gather a variety of flowers, which I put in various spots all over the house. That warmed her up a little. Then I gave her a giant card with a hand on the front that could be turned thumbs up or thumbs down. "Which way is it?" I asked her. She turned it thumbs up. I never said whether I was right or wrong, only that I felt badly about the night before. And so began a history of offenses I never knew how to clear up with her.

Had someone not shared with me later the secret of developing a lasting and intimate relationship, we might have joined the millions who seek divorce each year.

End every day with a clean slate—no offenses between the two of you.

Couples often ask me, "Where have we gone wrong?" "Why don't we feel romantic toward each other?" "How come we argue so much?" "Why do we avoid touching each other?" These problems are not primarily attributable to incompatibility, sexual problems, financial pressure, or any other surface issues. They are a direct result of *accumulated offenses*. If a husband and wife can understand how to maintain harmony by immediately working to clear up every hurtful offense between them, they can climb out of such common problems and even marriage's deepest pit —divorce.

HOW DID I GET DOWN HERE ANYWAY?

When a man treats his wife carelessly, she is usually offended far deeper than he realizes. She begins to close him out, and if he continues to hurt her feelings, she will separate herself from him mentally, emotionally, and physically. In other words, she doesn't want any contact in any way with him. Haven't you noticed how your wife clams up after you have insulted her? She not only avoids conversation, but also avoids being touched. A *wife simply will not respond to her husband when he continually hurts her feelings without "clearing the slate"—draining away her anger*.

Some people justify their reactions by saying, "But he/ she hurt my feelings." There's no such thing as hurt feelings, according to psychologist Dr. Henry Brandt. He says, "Let's call hurt feelings what they really are—anger." It isn't right for your wife to react in anger, but that's not the point of this book. Our goal as husbands should be to adjust our behavior so our wives won't have to react in anger.

To understand why your wife naturally "clams up" when you offend her, imagine yourself the proud owner of a new car. When you first drive that classy model into your driveway, every part of you says, "I love it." You love the smell, the feel, the look. Because you love the car, you polish it until it sparkles. You devote special time and care to it. However, a month later when the engine starts knocking, or the oil leaks, or the gleaming paint job suffers a few scratches, or the windshield wipers quit right in the middle of a rain storm, you become irritated with this "lemon" that you've bought. Soon you can think of seventy-two reasons to get rid of it. As long as it treats you right, you like it. But as soon as it starts to fall apart, you wish you'd never bought it, and soon you don't even want to be near it.

The same thing can happen with a job. Did you ever quit because you weren't happy with the boss or working conditions? I remember how much I loved one job until the boss offended me deeply. At that moment, my mind became tangled in a web of reasons to leave. Although I knew what was going on inside me, I couldn't seem to control my emotions. They had changed, and I wasn't as fond of the work as I had been. I eventually didn't want to show up or have anything to do with that job.

We tend to follow a natural pattern when we've been offended. Mentally, we are more alert to the flaws of the offender. Emotionally, we feel estranged. Physically, we avoid that person. And spiritually, we close out the person (Prov. 15:13).

I have watched my wife go through this process many times. When I played basketball that Valentine's evening instead of going home to her romantic candlelight dinner, she was so angry that she didn't want to talk to me. She didn't want to touch me or have me touch her. Have you ever put your arm around your wife after provoking her and felt her tighten up? You may have criticized her when that happened. But you need to accept the responsibility for her coldness and say, "I understand how you feel, and I don't blame you for not wanting me near you right now. What I did was wrong, and I ask your forgiveness." If your wife does not want you to touch her, if she has lost some of that romantic "spark" she once had for you, or if she is plotting ways to get away from you even for short periods of time, *you can be sure you have offended her and possibly "closed" her spirit.* (In my book, *The Key to Your Child's Heart*, I talk in detail about what "closes" a person's spirit and specific ways in which we can "reopen" it.)

A not-so-funny thing happened on the way to a party one evening. Norma teasingly said she planned to play a joke on the company president, a joke that would have embarrassed me. I couldn't believe she would consider such a thing, and I said, "Norma, you can't do that. I'm not going tonight if you really plan on doing it."

I stopped the car and with harshness and impatience yelled, "I would be too embarrassed to go there." She kidded around with me a little more and admitted she really wasn't serious, but my persistent harshness was too much for her (Prov. 15:4). Because I was so abusive, she began to cry. Realizing I had done the wrong thing, I tried to make it right. The more I talked, the worse it grew. At the party, whenever I glanced at her, she looked away. She was thinking of all the reasons her husband wasn't such a "great catch" anymore. It took days for me to reestablish harmony.

What does a man have to do to clear up offenses against his wife? How can he maintain harmony with her?

Harmony can be defined as the absence of unsettled offenses between the two of you.

When a real harmony and oneness exist between you and your wife, the two of you will want to relax and spend time talking. Your wife will be more agreeable. She will feel emotionally and physically attracted to you. But when you have offended her, she will probably *resist* you and *argue* with you.

Wives are often accused of being strong-willed and rebellious when, in reality, they're simply responding to their husbands' thoughtless abuses. They are sometimes accused of wrecking marriages because they have lost affectionate or romantic love for their husbands. Of course, husbands seldom realize that their insensitive behavior is what ushered the affection out the door.

It doesn't make much sense to withhold the necessary elements a plant needs (like air, water, soil, etc.) and then blame the plant for not thriving. However, many a man has labeled his wife sexually frigid for not wanting to be touched or have sex. But wives have often told me that when a woman is mistreated, she feels like a prostitute having physical relations with her husband. Sex is more than just physical—it involves every part of us. A woman must first know she is valued as a person and be in harmony with her husband before she can give herself freely in sex. She has to feel romantic love before *wholeheartedly* entering the sexual union in marriage. Without harmony, the sexual relationship between husband and wife will most certainly deteriorate.

Have you ever known the futility of trying to reach a woman mentally, emotionally, and physically after offending her?

Mark tried to reach out to Laurie, his estranged wife, but she wanted no part of him. He kept saying to her, "I miss you so much. I want to be near you. I love you." But she was *closed* to him emotionally. "Don't you see how you're hurting our daughter?" he said. "Don't you see what kind of reputation we're going to have by being separated?" He tried to appeal to her mentally, but she wouldn't listen. He had already gone too far—he had offended her too often and too severely—so her spirit completely shut him out of her life.

I asked him, "Are you willing to forgo touching Laurie

for the time being, to forgo wondering if she will ever again have emotional feelings for you, to forgo trying to reason with her mentally? Will you concentrate on clearing up your past offenses?

"If you will accept my counsel and reestablish a harmony with Laurie, she will mentally open up to you again. She'll gain new romantic love for you. Finally, she will desire to be near you again.

"This is the reality of life," I advised Mark. "In cases where a woman has fallen in love with another man or has been *severely* mistreated, it may take longer to win her back."

A man often becomes disgusted when his wife doesn't sparkle with romance any more, not realizing that he killed that sparkle with his hurtful ways.

What steps can a man take to rebuild a harmonious relationship with his wife?

FIVE WAYS TO LOVINGLY DRAIN ANGER FROM YOUR WIFE AND GAIN A LASTING AND LOVING RELATIONSHIP

1. *Endeavor to understand the ways you have hurt or offended your wife.* To help you avoid hurting your mate, I have included a list of ways a husband commonly offends his wife. (This list is on pages 93 to 99.) In the past, perhaps you haven't realized how deeply your actions were hurting her.

Ken and Sharon's story is a good example of how a man's insensitivity damaged a marriage. After eight years of marriage and three children, Sharon's once-petite figure was a little on the chubby side. Since Ken couldn't understand why she had not regained her slender figure after the birth of their third child, he found a number of "creative" ways to point out the extra poundage to Sharon. He tried to make her lose weight by lecturing, demanding, and bribing. He even threatened to cancel their vacation unless she lost weight. But nothing worked. She seemed powerless to comply.

Ken's continually critical, harsh attitude wounded Sharon. As a result, she slowly began to close him out of her life. She shut him out emotionally, and resisted when he demanded sex, excusing herself because of headaches or fatigue. His occasional jabs, "Do you realize you had two desserts for dinner tonight?" and his overbearing personality continually pressured her, making her more nervous and increasing her desire to eat. Ken was totally unaware of what he was doing to her. There was no way he could really understand her. "If you want to lose weight," he said, "you just decide to do it!"

Since Sharon had little or no interest in pleasing Ken, she might have been subconsciously punishing him by staying overweight. Quite by accident, Ken did one thing that finally motivated Sharon to lose weight. He called her long distance while on a business trip and said,"Honey, as I've been away from you and the kids these past few days, I've had a lot of time to think. I know I've never been able to face it before, but I've been judgmental and offensive to each of you. In fact, I can see now that *I've* been the one out of control. In many ways, my crummy attitude is worse than anything you've done to me.

"What I plan to do is to stop pestering you about losing weight, and to spend the rest of my life focusing on how I can work on being a better friend and husband. I want to concentrate on learning how to love you for who you are, not criticizing you for not measuring up to my standards. I want you to know that you're free from demands from me to change and that I love you just the way you are."

After a few stunned seconds, Sharon responded, "You know, every time you demanded that I lose weight, your attitude made me want to run to the refrigerator and eat everything in it! I never had any desire to please you in this area. But now that you say I'm free to do whatever I want and I sense you mean it, I actually have a greater desire to lose weight"—which she did by losing over seventy pounds in the next few months.

When Ken began to recognize that his criticism was wounding his wife, he was on the path to a restored relationship.

2. *Admit the fact that you've participated in weakening your marriage.* Men, what you're about to read may be very difficult for you to believe or even accept. I want you to keep in mind that this whole book, *If Only He Knew*, is directed to *you*. It's not intended for a woman to read, and it doesn't specifically apply to what she needs to do to restore or rebuild a relationship. Steve Scott and I took the time to write an entire book for her, *For Better or for Best*, to point out areas where her attitudes and actions can serve to strengthen or weaken your marriage.

But let's get back to the crucial point you need to consider: *If your marriage is continually under stress, is filled with strife, and is bordering on collapse, you've been participating in weakening it.*

When I first heard what you're about to read, I squirmed and fought and argued against the whole idea for at least a month. I want you to experience whatever emotions are natural to you as you read the statement in the box below. If you react strongly, I understand why. In spite of my initial opposition, I ultimately realized that there was more truth in it than I wanted to admit. You may want to react like I did and spend long hours trying to disprove it. But let's face it together.

> IF A COUPLE HAS BEEN MARRIED FOR MORE THAN FIVE YEARS, ANY PERSISTENT DISHAR-MONY IN THEIR MARRIAGE RELATIONSHIP IS USUALLY ATTRIBUTABLE TO THE HUSBAND'S LACK OF UNDERSTANDING AND APPLYING GENUINE LOVE.

I'm not suggesting that the husband is solely responsible for all disharmony in a marriage. Day-to-day conflicts can arise because of his wife's physical exhaustion, health problems, or overloaded schedules. On any given day, she may respond negatively to her husband due to a headache, a disturbing phone call from her father, or any number of other temporary upsets. Certainly, the husband is not to blame for these occasional problems.

Perhaps you have married a woman who believes her father or mother hated her, rejected her, or otherwise never "blessed" her. (For insight into the powerful biblical concept of "blessing" others, see my book written with John Trent, *The Blessing*, which talks about the tremendous benefit of growing up with parental love and acceptance, their "blessing," and the incredible damage that can come from living without it.) If your wife didn't receive her parents' blessing, you're probably going to experience a woman who tends to be critical, judgmental, or otherwise difficult to live with.

In situations like that, I certainly can't say that daily disharmony is all the fault of the husband. But I can say that biblically speaking, you're still responsible for the disharmony in your home. Does this sound confusing?

The Scriptures teach that the husband is charged with the responsibility of overseeing the welfare of his wife and children. In fact, Ephesians 5:23 says that he is to love his wife as Christ loved the church and actually sacrificed Himself so others might live. After five years of marriage if a husband has failed to understand or seek help for the major causes of their disharmony, he either doesn't understand what genuine love is or has chosen to ignore God's command to shepherd his family wisely.

During a lecture I was giving, one man violently reacted to this concept, saying, "When a woman gets out of line, I think you ought to knock her up against the wall!"

"Throw him out!" a woman in the meeting shouted back.

His reaction shocked me at first, but I later discovered that he and his wife were in one of those "marriage pits." Since he was trying to scare and convince his wife into believing that all the problems in their marriage were her fault, accepting any part of my statement would have destroyed his line of reasoning—and forced him to deal with the pain he had caused her and the guilt he sought so hard to repress.

I know of at least three types of men who vigorously resist accepting this concept I've shared here:

A man who is bitter over his wife leaving him. He would have to admit the failure of the marriage was at least partially his fault, and that admission is almost too much to ask of him.

A man with a close relative or friend whose wife has divorced him. "It couldn't have been my brother's fault. You never met his terrible wife." (Don't forget, though, most of what you know about that "terrible wife" you learned from your brother. He may be a great brother but a very insensitive husband.)

A man having an affair. It's just too hard for him to blame

*himself for a frigid or nagging wife. He feels she was enough to
drive him into another woman's arms and explains away his
own error and insensitivity.* Sondra
2,

I tried in vain to find an exception to this concept by
asking the question, "How can this be true when . . . ?" For
example, I looked at two "exceptions" I had heard about
recently.

"How can this be true when my neighbor down the street
is so hard to get along with that no man could live with
her negative moods day after day?" and "How could you
possibly blame Jim for flirting when his wife, Jane, doesn't
respond to him sexually?" I soon discovered that I couldn't
disprove this concept with these two types of objections.
One uses a hypothetical situation, the other a second hand
example.

These two "exceptions" don't work because vital facts
are missing. What was it that developed the bad attitude
in our neighbor? It may have been her father or her husband
or any number of causes. In any case, the husband has the
biblical responsibility to find out what is causing it (even
if it's him) and begin to take steps to solve it.

Hypothetical situations leave out the context of the problem. Excusing Jim's flirting behavior because his wife is
sexually frigid also ignores the fact that Jim may have caused
her to close her spirit, which resulted in their sexual problems. Not only that, but other people's errant behavior still
doesn't give anyone a license to be irresponsible.

DOES THIS WHOLE CONCEPT SOUND ONE-SIDED?

I knew by Norma's facial expression that I had offended her one morning. I immediately said, "I understand what I just said was too harsh, and I shouldn't have said it. I would like to ask you to forgive me."

"Okay, I'll forgive you," she said.

I thought to myself, *You know, this whole thing is one-sided here. It seems like all the pressure is on me to act right. What about her?*

So I said, "Hey, how come I'm always the one that has to ask forgiveness when I do something wrong? Why don't you ask me to forgive you anymore? This is one-sided, isn't it?"

Then she looked at me and said, "I'd be happy to admit where I am wrong and seek your forgiveness *if* I have offended you."

"Well, that's just too much! What an arrogant statement. What a terribly selfish thing to say," I said. "There are lots of things you have done to offend me. I can't remember the last time you admitted you were wrong and sought my forgiveness."

"Well, what are some of my offenses?" she asked.

"Give me a minute and I'll think of a lot of them," I said.

"Well, what are they!" she asked again.

"Just a minute and I'll think of some," I said, stalling for time.

I thought and thought, but I couldn't come up with even one. I told myself, *This can't be true.* But I couldn't think of a thing she had done to offend me.

Finally I said, "But I can think of some things I'd like

to see you change about yourself."

"Well, what are they?"

"Even though we've been married five years, I'm going to come up with the first exception to this thing of it being all my fault. (I was pleased with myself.) There are some times when you don't respect me and you don't honor me as a special person in your life. Sometimes your words are cutting and disrespectful . . . *now how is that my responsibility?*"

We sat down at the kitchen table and started going through each item. It took only ten minutes for us to figure out that every time she had been disrespectful to me I had either rolled out of bed grouchy or been critical of her most of the day. I hadn't earned her respect. It was amazing. All three things I had felt *she* should change were a direct result of *my* failure to love her in a genuine way. Once we talked, Norma was more than willing to apologize for her offensive reactions. She freely admitted her reactions to my behavior were wrong. But for the first time, I saw clearly how much my insensitive actions had provided a backdrop for her negative reactions!

Now I have to admit the whole episode left a bad taste in my mouth. Even today, when I'm tired or a little down, I think to myself, *This is crazy. I shouldn't even tell people this because it'll make wives run all over their husbands.* But just the opposite is true. When a man treats his wife with gentleness, when he is loving and understanding, and when he does most of the things we describe in this book, she will respond to him on every level. She'll desire intimate conversation with him, she'll feel emotional love for him, and she'll respond to him sexually. The only exception, as I mentioned before, occurs when a wife is romantically involved with another man.

In Search of an Exception

Recently, I talked with a man. After years of raising the children, his wife had reluctantly gone back to working part-time. Soon she was getting so many pats on the back for her hard work habits and positive attitude that she was asked to become a full-time employee. And that's when the problems began with her husband.

Now she was too tired to prepare him the kind of dinners he was used to having and all she wanted to do was talk about work. Finally, his anger built up to the point that he lashed out at her, "Where are your priorities, anyway? Isn't our marriage important to you any more?"

Not wanting to inflame him further, she tried to avoid the conversation with a half-hearted response that she'd try a little harder to have dinner on time. Unfortunately, that wasn't the only thing wrong, and soon their marriage had deteriorated so much that they were in my office for counseling as a last step before undertaking divorce proceedings.

When I met this couple, I asked them several questions, the same questions the husband could have asked his wife if he had known how to bring healing to their marriage. I asked them, "On a scale of 0 to 10, where has your marriage been over the past several years, overall?" He responded with a "6 or 7" and then after a long pause, she said it had been a "2, at best."

Then I asked, "Where would you two like to be?" Both of them agreed that what they had married for was to have "a 10 as often as possible, but at least an 8."

Then I asked them a key question, "What would it take to move your relationship up to an 8 and on the way to a 10?" Almost immediately, this man's wife said, "He'd have to talk to me more. . . ." But before she could finish her sentence, her husband cut her short and said, "I *do* talk to you; *you're* the one who is too tired to talk because of working all the time."

After his angry outburst, his wife's response was typical of what I have heard time and time again in counseling sessions. She said to him, "What you call conversation is really verbal abuse, and I'm tired of it. You don't want to talk to me. You just want to lecture me about all the things I'm doing wrong. Well, not everyone thinks I'm such a loser! People at work think I'm worth something. Why do you think I enjoy it there so much?"

For almost twenty years, any conversation this man had with his wife had been an opportunity for him to demand what he could have asked for nicely or to criticize another area of her character or appearance. When his wife was finally around some positive people, she blossomed like a flower—and didn't want anything to do with her insensitive husband as a result.

Fortunately, there was still a spark of love in their marriage and they were both willing to make a decision to try to make it work. After several counseling sessions, he understood and admitted for the first time that he had been offensive, angry, and a poor communicator. And even though she continues to work, now several years later, their marriage relationship has tripled in terms of mutual satisfaction.

If only he had known years ago what it took for her to want to spend time with him, he could have avoided years of unnecessary pain. He needed to realize that wisdom dwells in those people willing to be corrected and even seeking to get error out of their lives.

I realize how difficult it is for us to admit we are wrong. One night Norma and I were lying in bed when I said something obnoxious to her. She closed me out, and though

I wanted to restore our relationship, I was too proud to say anything.

The words stuck in my throat. I wanted to say, "Norma, I was wrong about what I just said." I tried, but the words just wouldn't come. I decided to roll over and go to sleep, thinking it would be easier to admit my mistake in the morning. Throughout the night I woke up, feeling more and more eager to admit I was wrong and feeling worse and worse about what I had done.

By morning I could admit my mistake, and our relationship was restored. But do you realize what I had done to Norma and what many of us men are capable of doing to our wives? Not only do we offend them on the one hand, but we leave them to suffer for hours (or even weeks or months) before being willing to make things right. Over the years, hundreds of wives have told me that if their husbands had come to them earlier and dealt with problem issues, they would have been spared double the pain—feeling the hurt of the initial offense and then having to wait for restoration.

One of the quickest ways to restore your marriage is to demonstrate genuine conviction and sorrow for seeing such a valuable person as your wife treated in a dishonoring way.

3. *Express genuine sorrow to your wife whenever you offend her.* One of the most dramatic examples of the power of this particular point was shown to me by an All-Pro defensive player on an NFL championship team.

At a professional football conference where I was speaking, I walked into the coffee shop and witnessed this player and his wife in the middle of a very tense and tearful discussion. Knowing how big and powerful these athletes are—especially when they're angry—I was a little reluctant when he called me over to the table and asked if I would talk with them a few minutes.

He had been upset with his wife because she was too tired after their long airplane flight to go out with some friends after the evening meeting. Her reluctance displeased him, and he shamed her in front of the other couple. He was angry with her all night, too. Now, over breakfast, he was trying to make up and she wasn't responding.

When they walked into the coffee shop, he tried to put his arm around her, and she pulled away, embarrassing him in the process. Before they knew it, they were in the middle of another fight. That's when he called me over to the table. "I don't want to spend the whole week like this. What can we do?" he said.

I encouraged him to understand how hurtful it was for her to hear his harsh put-downs in front of the other players and wives.

And he said, "Well, it was wrong of her, too. She could have stayed up for another hour. We're at a conference, and this is a place to have fun!"

Then she said, "This is so typical. He's always thinking about having fun with his friends and doesn't really care about me. I was tired from getting us packed and the kids off to my folks, and he got mad because he didn't want to go without me."

The tension level between the two of them was so high by this point that it could have reheated the coffee in front of us. Other people seated around us were painfully aware of the scene between them.

I tried something with them that I had never done before (nor since), and the immediate results amazed all of us. I asked him to pay attention to what I was about to say to her and said, "If you don't want to be upset all week, would you be willing to do something like this? For just a minute, let me pretend that I'm you."

I reached across the table, and I put my hand gently on

top of hers. I looked her right in the eyes, and I said in a soft voice, "What I said to you in front of our friends last night was really wrong. I know it embarrassed you and really offended you. You're just too valuable to be treated like this. In fact, I don't even know how you put up with me like you do. You may not be able to respond right now, and I'll try and understand if you can't, but if you could, I'd love it if you forgave me. I know I don't deserve it, and I know I may blow it again. But I want you to know with all my heart that I don't want to hurt you, and I don't like living this way."

I pulled my hand away and sat back. Immediately, tears welled up in her eyes, and her facial muscles and her entire body seemed to relax.

"Do you see what's happening to your wife here?" I asked my NFL friend. As he looked at her, tears began to show in his eyes as well, and I said to him, "Can you see how your wife would respond if you would treat her with tenderness and be willing to admit the times that you're wrong?"

She immediately turned to him and said, "Yeah, but you could never do that!"

"Oh, yes I could," he said in an irritated tone of voice. Almost instantly he was feeling defensive again, and her facial muscles tightened up again.

For the next hour and a half he practiced—with his arm around her or gently holding her hand—how to speak to her and ask her forgiveness in a soft, genuine way when he had wronged her. On the football field, this fellow had spent years learning to "never give an inch." Now he began to discover that in marriage, when he wronged his wife he needed to take off the shoulder pads and admit that he was wrong. Two years later, I saw this same couple at another conference, and their marriage had never been better because of practicing this one principle.

My wife, Norma, has told me time and time again how much she appreciates seeing my genuine sorrow when I have hurt her. "How do you put up with me? How do you live with me? You deserve the medal of honor for staying with me. You deserve the purple heart. You are an amazing woman to live with such an insensitive man." Sincere words like those express my repentant spirit and soothe our relationship.

I asked one woman, "After your husband has verbally abused you, would you appreciate it if he admitted he was wrong and expressed sorrow that you were hurting? What would you do if he said, 'How do you put up with such a crumb like me, as insensitive as I am?'"

"I'd call the cops," she said.

I repeated in amazement, "You'd call the cops?"

"Yes, because I'd know that there was an imposter in the house," she replied.

I have had wives say to me, "My husband will never admit when he's wrong. He's too proud." Yet I meet husbands everywhere who are willing to admit their offenses if their wives are patient enough to help them understand *how* they have offended them.

Before we go on, let's review why each of these major steps greatly contributes to restoring harmony in the home. First, persistent disharmony is almost always reduced by you sincerely endeavoring to understand the ways you have offended your wife—literally trying to understand the depth of the hurt she has felt by your actions.

Second, you need to be willing to admit to yourself specifically what you have done to weaken your relationship. The greater your understanding of her suffering, the easier it can be for you to see what you've done wrong, and to take the third and often hardest step—expressing your sincere sorrow for your offensive actions. The more specific, the better when it comes to sharing how you have been wrong. This helps your spouse realize that you really do understand how she has suffered. And it leads to the fourth important aspect of restoring the relationship, seeking her forgiveness.

4. *Seek her forgiveness for your offensive behavior.* A woman needs a man who *understands* the *depth* of her grief after his hurtful behavior. Wives have said to me, "If only my husband knew how much I feel those words that he says so glibly and harshly. If only he knew how long they stay with me." Harsh words can stay with a woman for years.

A woman loves to hear her man say, "Will you forgive me?" And when she verbalizes, "Yes, you're forgiven," she is freer to restore her side of the relationship. However, if her husband simply says, "Oh, honey, I'm sorry," it's not always enough. He might be able to get away with it if he says it in a tender and gentle way, but a woman really needs to hear, "Will you forgive me?" That proves her husband values her half of the relationship. A flippant "I'm sorry" may mean "I'm sorry I got caught" or "I'm sorry to have to put up with your insensitivity." It usually doesn't restore the relationship to oneness and harmony.

Initially, your wife may appear unable or unwilling to grant forgiveness for any number of reasons. Perhaps she doesn't really believe you, or she thinks you really don't understand her real hurts or disappointment. She may even bluntly say, "No, I won't forgive you..." or "Give me some time..." or, "When I see a change in you, *maybe....*" All of these are responses of a woman who has been deeply hurt, and all of them might tempt you to react in anger or try to verbally attack her for not forgiving you.

As hard as it may be to restrain yourself, reacting in anger to her statements can only drive her further away. Very often, a woman needs a track record of demonstrated forgiveness before emotionally feeling like granting it to her husband. She may make the decision to forgive, but it may take her some time to feel forgiving. That's why husbands need to be aware of something very unique about women.

Most women respond to a husband who genuinely and *persistently* seeks to restore their relationship. It may take an hour or several hours of "cooling off" and then coming back to talk. But like the situation of the NFL football player, a wife will usually respond positively to a man who gently and persistently asks her forgiveness. And that is why the next point is so important.

5. *Let her see your consistent and sincere efforts to correct offensive actions or words.* This is another way of saying, "Repent." For the Greeks, the word "repent" literally meant "to turn around." It means that you are to change your way of thinking or acting to the way Christ thought and acted (Luke 17:3–5).

A woman isn't impressed with a man who seeks forgiveness or admits he is wrong and then continues to hurt her year after year in the same areas. Words are nice, but they are not enough.

Attitudes, not words or actions, often harm a woman the most. When she *sees* her husband's attitudes changing, she is more willing to hope again and to be open with him and accept him into an intimate relationship. Otherwise, she'll keep him closed off for fear of being offended again.

People of the Lie

One of the most important words in the boxed statement on page 80 is the word "usually." It means that a broken relationship is not always attributable to the husband. After more than twenty years of working with couples all across the country, I have discovered only one situation that makes it more difficult and, in some very rare cases, nearly impossible for a wife to respond to her husband's genuine love when he consistently applies it.

This situation arises when a woman has had prolonged anger in her life. She has spent years being bitter and resentful toward her mom and dad or others, and as a result she has developed into a habitual liar and someone who has deep-seated feelings of inferiority. These three deadly ingredients—unresolved resentment, habitual lying, and deep-seated inferiority, when mixed together over the years—can create what M. Scott Peck calls a "Person of the Lie." These people are unwilling to recognize or deal with the hurts they cause others, and they steadfastly refuse to admit any wrong in their own lives.

Remember, it is most unusual for a wife to be unresponsive to her husband's sincere love. Before you jump to any conclusions or say to yourself, "Now that's better. He's finally talking about *my wife*," let's look at some of the ways (more than one hundred of them) that a husband can offend his wife and can contribute to her developing anger, resentment, or other negative emotions or behavior.

When a husband recognizes that he has offended his wife in any of these ways, he needs to clear it up in order to restore the relationship. Why not ask your wife to check the ones that are true of you?

1. Ignoring her.
2. Not valuing her opinions.
3. Showing more attention to other people than her.
4. Not listening to her or not understanding what she feels is important.
5. Closing her out by not talking or listening to her (the silent treatment).
6. Being easily distracted when she's trying to talk.

7. Not scheduling special time to be with her.
8. Not being open to talk about things that you do not understand.
9. Not being open to talk about things that she does not understand.
10. Not giving her a chance to voice her opinion on decisions that affect the whole family.
11. Disciplining her by being angry or silent.
12. Making jokes about areas of her life.
13. Making sarcastic statements about her.
14. Insulting her in front of others.
15. Coming back with quick retorts.
16. Giving harsh admonitions.
17. Using careless words before you think through how they will affect her.
18. Nagging her in harshness.
19. Rebuking her before giving her a chance to explain a situation.
20. Raising your voice at her.
21. Making critical comments with no logical basis.
22. Swearing or using foul language in her presence.
23. Correcting her in public.
24. Being tactless when pointing out her weaknesses or blind spots.
25. Reminding her angrily that you warned her not to do something.
26. Having disgusted or judgmental attitudes.
27. Pressuring her when she is already feeling low or offended.
28. Lecturing her when she needs to be comforted, encouraged, or treated gently.
29. Breaking promises without any explanation or without being asked to be released from the promise.
30. Telling her how wonderful other women are and com-

paring her to other women.

31. Holding resentment about something she did and tried to make right.
32. Being disrespectful to her family and relatives.
33. Coercing her into an argument.
34. Correcting or punishing her in anger for something for which she's not guilty.
35. Not praising her for something she did well, even if she did it for you.
36. Treating her like a little child.
37. Being rude to her or to other people in public, like restaurant personnel or clerks.
38. Being unaware of her needs.
39. Being ungrateful.
40. Not trusting her.
41. Not approving of what she does or how she does it.
42. Not being interested in her own personal growth.
43. Being inconsistent or having double standards (doing things you won't allow her to do).
44. Not giving her advice when she really needs it and asks for it.
45. Not telling her that you love her.
46. Having prideful and arrogant attitudes in general.
47. Not giving daily encouragement.
48. Failing to include her in a conversation when you are with other people.
49. Failing to spend quantity or quality time with her when you're at a party.
50. "Talking her down"—continuing to discuss or argue a point just to prove you're right.
51. Ignoring her around the house as if she weren't a member of the family.
52. Not taking time to listen to what she believes is important as soon as you come home from work.

53. Ignoring her at social gatherings.
54. Not attending church as a family.
55. Failure to express honestly what you think her innermost feelings are.
56. Showing more excitement for work and other activities than for her.
57. Being impolite at mealtime.
58. Having sloppy manners around the house and in front of others.
59. Not inviting her out on special romantic dates from time to time (just the two of you).
60. Not helping her with the children just before mealtimes or during times of extra stress.
61. Not volunteering to help her with the dishes occasionally—or with cleaning the house.
62. Making her feel stupid when she shares an idea about your work or decisions that need to be made.
63. Making her feel unworthy for desiring certain furniture or insurance or other material needs for herself and the family.
64. Not being consistent with the children; not taking an interest in playing with them and spending quality and quantity time with them.
65. Not showing public affection for her, like holding her hand or putting your arm around her (you seem to be embarrassed to be with her).
66. Not sharing your life with her, like your ideas or your feelings (e.g., what's going on at work).
67. Not being the spiritual leader of the home.
68. Demanding that she submit to you.
69. Demanding that she be involved with you sexually when you are not in harmony.
70. Being unwilling to admit you were wrong.

71. Resisting whenever she shares one of your "blind spots."

72. Being too busy with work and activities.

73. Not showing compassion and understanding for her and the children when there is real need.

74. Not planning for the future, making her very insecure.

75. Being stingy with money, making her feel like she's being paid a salary—and not much at all.

76. Wanting to do things that embarrass her sexually.

77. Reading sexual magazines in front of her or the children.

78. Forcing her to make many of the decisions regarding the checkbook and bills.

79. Forcing her to handle bill collectors and overdue bills.

80. Not letting her lean on your gentleness and strength from time to time.

81. Not allowing her to fail—always feeling like you have to lecture her.

82. Refusing to let her be a woman.

83. Criticizing her womanly characteristics or sensitivity as being weak.

84. Spending too much money and getting the family too far into debt.

85. Not having a sense of humor and not joking about things together.

86. Not telling her how important she is to you.

87. Not sending her special love letters from time to time.

88. Forgetting special dates like anniversaries and birthdays.

89. Not defending her when somebody else is complaining or tearing her down (especially if it's one of your relatives or friends).

90. Not putting your arm around her and hugging her

when she's in need of comfort.

91. Not bragging to other people about her.
92. Being dishonest.
93. Discouraging her for trying to better herself, either through education or physical fitness.
94. Continuing distasteful or harmful habits, like coming home drunk.
95. Not treating her as if "Handle With Care" were stamped on her forehead.
96. Ignoring her relatives and the people who are important to her.
97. Taking her for granted, assuming that "a woman's work is never done" around the house.
98. Not including her in future plans until the last minute.
99. Never doing little unexpected things for her.
100. Not treating her like an intellectual equal.
101. Looking at her as a weaker individual in general.
102. Being preoccupied with your own goals and needs, making her feel like she and the children do not count.
103. Threatening never to let her do something again because she made some mistake in the past.
104. Criticizing her behind her back. (This is really painful for her if she hears about your criticism from someone else.)
105. Blaming her for things in your relationship that are clearly your failure.
106. Not being aware of her physical limitations, treating her like a man by roughhousing with her or making her carry heavy objects.
107. Losing patience or getting angry with her when she can't keep up with your schedule or physical stamina.
108. Acting like you're a martyr if you go along with her opinions.

109. Sulking when she challenges your comments.
110. Joining too many organizations which exclude her and the children.
111. Failing to repair items around the house.
112. Watching too much TV and therefore neglecting her and the children.
113. Demanding that she sit and listen to your point of view when she needs to be taking care of the children's needs.
114. Insisting on lecturing her in order to convey what you believe are important points.
115. Humiliating her with words and actions, saying things like "I can't stand living in a pigpen."
116. Not taking the time to prepare her to enjoy sexual intimacy.
117. Spending money extravagantly without helping those less fortunate.
118. Avoiding family activities that the children enjoy.
119. Taking vacations that are primarily for your pleasure, like fishing or hunting, while preventing her from shopping and doing the things she enjoys doing.
120. Not letting her get away from the children just to be with friends, go shopping for special items, or have a weekend away with her friends.
121. Being unwilling to join her in the things she enjoys like shopping, going out for coffee and dessert at a restaurant, etc.
122. Not understanding the boring chores a housewife does: like picking up clothes and toys all day long, wiping runny noses, putting on and taking off muddy boots and jackets, washing and ironing, etc., etc.

CAN A WEAKENED MARRIAGE RELATIONSHIP REALLY BE TRACED TO THE HUSBAND'S LACK OF GENUINE LOVE?

I want to emphasize the fact that *only after five years* of marriage is a husband responsible for the prolonged disharmony in his marriage. When you marry a woman, you inherit the way she was treated by her father, her mother, her brothers and sisters, and even her friends. She is the sum total of her environment, her associations, and her life as a single person. Here again let's keep in mind that God called the man to be the leader in nurturing his wife and children. If he leads in offensive, harsh, angry behavior, he will reap the results in a weakened or fractured marriage. On the other hand, he can also set a positive tone, which is encouraged by many suggestions in this book.

The main problem that we men have to overcome is our *lack* of knowledge and skills to nurture (Eph. 5:28–29) our wives to a level from which we can enjoy a growing, loving, and intimate relationship with them. We, too, are the sum total of our environment, etc.

You may be thinking thoughts similar to those Mike had when he challenged me on this whole concept.

"Now wait a minute," Mike said. "That can't be true."

I assured him, "I know, it's hard to believe."

"Well, take my wife, Carol, for example," he said. "She has divorced me, but you can't tell me that the problems we had in our relationship can all be traced to my failure to love her. I just can't buy that."

To prove my point, I said, "Give me an example— something you didn't like about her—and we'll see if we can check this thing out."

"Take this one example," he said, confident that he could

disprove this concept. "On our wedding night we had sexual relations. She was turned off by the whole experience and from that day on, for over twenty years, she never really enjoyed our sex life. She never initiated it. She didn't even want to be involved. It was always at my initiative.

"I felt she was more of an object that wasn't really involved in this relationship. How would I be the cause of that? On our wedding night, she changed on me!"

Mike had dated Carol for three years. So I asked how he treated her during those years.

"Well, okay," he said.

"Mike, I happen to know that it wasn't okay. You and I both know that you had a reputation of being mean and extremely insensitive to her. Do you remember some of the things you did?"

When he admitted that he did remember, I said, "You really hurt her feelings. During all those years that you dated her, did you ever clear up your offenses with her?"

"No, I didn't. I didn't know how to do it. I didn't know what to do," he said.

"Why did she marry you—to get away from her family?"

"Right."

"Then the first night she realized that sex wasn't that great. And do you know why?" I asked. "Because you two weren't in harmony. Besides this fact, did you prepare her for sex?" I explained that many women tell me they need as much as three days' preparation for sex, romantically and emotionally, before they can respond to their husbands. A woman is sort of like an iron and a man is like a light bulb. She *warms up* to the sexual expression, while he *turns on* immediately.

"Did you ever clear your conscience with her? Did you ever clear those past offenses when you were married?" I asked him.

"No, I never did." Mike had never admitted he was wrong.

"Did you criticize your wife a lot?" I asked. Mike's head sank lower and lower. He even admitted that he once told her all their problems were her fault. After a few minutes, tears appeared in his eyes because he realized how insensitive, cruel, and harsh he had been for all those years.

The chart on pages 104–107 will provide some additional illustrations to help you discover how you might have contributed to a weaker marriage relationship. (This chart was devised by Ken Nair, a marriage and family lecturer/counselor.) If you need help, you have an expert in your own home—your wife. You may be amazed at how well she remembers your unloving words and actions. However, many wives say they are afraid of their husbands, afraid to be honest for fear they'll be *rejected* or *criticized* for being illogical, too sensitive, or unforgiving.

IF YOU REACT TO THIS IDEA, YOU'RE NOT ALONE. MANY WIVES AND SINGLE WOMEN JOIN YOU

I explained this concept to an older woman whose husband had left her, after many years of marriage, for a younger woman. She resisted the idea that I could trace their broken relationship to her husband's failure.

"Oh, this is ridiculous. Everyone knows it's a fifty-fifty deal. I'm just as much responsible as he was," she argued.

"Well, I'm looking for my first exception. I would certainly appreciate it if you would explain to me where you were wrong in the relationship," I told her.

An hour later, she realized that if her husband had treated her differently, she would have responded much differently during those years. We traced everything he had accused her of to his failure to love her.

Some men (including me) have said this material is dangerous because it will make women irresponsible. They panic because they are afraid their wives will accuse them of things their wives really are guilty of in their marriage relationship. I can understand the panic. In general, the concept provokes us to rage because it reveals our irresponsibility as husbands, and we just can't take it—especially at first. Believe me, I know and understand the fight that might be going on inside you at this moment. However, if someone really thinks through this concept, it actually makes the husband and wife *more* responsible for their actions, not less.

Some single women also react negatively to this concept at first. For example, I overheard two of my editors discussing the concepts in this book; one was single and the other married.

"I just can't believe that some of the ideas in that book are good," said Debi, a twenty-five-year-old single woman "I don't believe part of it—like women are more emotional."

"Just wait until you're married," Judy told her. "In a year and a half of marriage, my husband and I have run into many of the problems discussed in Gary's book."

"Some of the generalizations bother me, though," Debi continued. "I don't feel that women in general are more sensitive and men more logical. I don't think you're more sensitive, because I've seen you at work. I know you."

"But it's different in a marriage," Judy said. "Just the other day when my husband was reading a chapter I had edited, he said, 'Hey, I think you're letting your thoughts creep into this book!' because the example was almost an identical account of a discussion we had recently." If this

HOW A HUSBAND'S LACK OF GENUINE LOVE

HUSBAND'S ACTIONS

Husband's Lack of Genuine Love	Amplified
UNRELIABLE	Lets time slip by unnoticed.
UNTRUSTING AND CONDEMNING	Has an attitude of superiority in finances. Demands the control of all money. Won't let his wife know about their financial status. Feels certain his wife would bankrupt him if she were given the chance.
ANGRY AND DEMANDING	In anger, over-reacts to children and others. Doesn't like to be inconvenienced by family. Sets standards too difficult for children to meet.
INSENSITIVE AND UNKIND	Uses hurtful words to others. Uses his wife or others as his source of humor.
INATTENTIVE AND THOUGHTLESS AND UNTRUST-WORTHY	Preoccupied with personal concerns. Dismisses others' personal feelings as unrealistic or invalid—if he acknowledges them at all. Family's reputation has been damaged by his lack of consideration for others.
UNCARING AND IRRESPONSIBLE	Doesn't seem to care about his family's needs. Seems to think the only obligation he has to the family is financial.

WEAKENS A MARRIAGE RELATIONSHIP

RESULT *Wife's Offensive Habits*	WIFE'S RESPONSES *Amplified*
NAGGING	Repeatedly reminds her husband about things that need attention, with illustrations of his past wrongs and forgetfulness.
IMPULSIVE SPENDER	Spends money as though it were very easily obtained. Seems irresponsible with money when it comes into her possession. Uses credit cards without concern.
PERMISSIVE WITH CHILDREN	Makes excuses for children's disobedience to husband and keeps secrets from him about their conduct.
TOO EMOTIONAL	Cries often and is easily hurt. Holds on to hurts for a long time. Able to recall past offenses in detail.
DOMINATING	Answers all questions, even those directed to her husband. Makes the decisions in the home and assumes responsibility for disciplining the children.
NAGGING	Repeatedly reminds her husband about things that need attention, with illustrations of his past wrongs.

CAN YOU IDENTIFY WITH ANY OF

THINGS A HUSBAND DISLIKES AND CRITICIZES IN HIS WIFE

1. She wants to be with her mother more than with him
2. She's lazy around the house

3. She's sexually frigid

4. She's sneaky

5. She's overly critical of the way he spends money
6. She avoids doing activities with him

7. She makes him feel like a nobody
8. She's afraid of speaking in front of groups
9. She yells at the kids in the morning

10. She's inflexible, always gets offended
11. She's independent
12. She's rebellious (unsubmissive)
13. She's disrespectful to him
14. She's snappy, angry
15. She reacts negatively to his friends

16. She's naggy

17. She's afraid of moving
18. She talks too much on the telephone
19. She's too lenient with the children
20. She reacts negatively to his relatives
21. She's too strict with the children
22. She's unwilling to pray with him

THESE TYPICAL CONFLICTS IN MARRIAGE?

COMMON EVIDENCE OF THE HUSBAND'S FAILURE TO GENUINELY LOVE HIS WIFE

1. He's overly critical and non-communicative
2. He's critical of how she keeps a house, a demanding perfectionist
3. He offends her by his harshness, is demanding, and offends the children
4. He's critical, judgmental, harsh, unyielding, insensitive to the needs of the children, stubborn, overly argumentative
5. He's irresponsible with money, extravagant
6. He's critical, not fun-loving, non-communicative, unwilling to shop or stop for a cup of coffee with her
7. He's harsh, offends her severely
8. He's critical of her grammar or speaking ability
9. He's undisciplined, neglects the training of the children, and does not help get them off to school
10. He rejects her and is overly critical of her
11. He's too possessive and critical of her
12. He has severely offended her and has not cleared it up
13. He's harsh and avoids her when with other people
14. He has severely offended her and broken promises
15. He prefers his friends over hers and defends his friends over hers
16. He doesn't assume his responsibility or is inattentive or untrustworthy
17. He makes sudden changes or is too impulsive
18. He isn't talking with her enough
19. He's too strict with the children
20. He prefers his relatives over hers
21. He's too lenient with the children
22. He has been offending her without clearing it up

section of the book doesn't do anything more than stimulate you to try and find an exception to the rule, it will be worthwhile. And if five years from now we discover hundreds of exceptions, the experience will still not have been damaging, because you and I need to become more responsible, loving partners, no matter what our wives do. That is the basis for genuine love—*doing what is right no matter what the other person does or says.*

Genuine love motivates us to build a relationship primarily for the other person's sake, and when we do that, we gain because we have a better relationship to enjoy.

FOR PERSONAL REFLECTION

1. What should we do if our mates offend us? Luke 17:3–4.
2. What attitude should we have when we rebuke an offender? Galations 6:1; Proverbs 15:1.

6

What No Woman Can Resist

"Let no unwholesome word proceed from your mouth, but only such a word as is good for edification."

Ephesians 4:29

The crunch of corn chips distracted my attention from the Saturday afternoon football game. I watched in amazement as my wife and three children began to eat their sandwiches and drink their Cokes while I sat only a couple of feet away without a bite to eat.

Why didn't she make me a sandwich? I asked myself. *I'm the sole bread winner, and I'm being ignored as if I didn't exist.* I cleared my throat loudly to catch my wife's attention. When that didn't work, I became so irritated that I walked into the kitchen, got the bread out, and made my own sandwich. When I sat back down in front of the TV, Norma didn't say a word nor did I. But I kept wondering, *If women are so sensitive, how come she didn't know I wanted a sandwich? If women are so alert, why didn't she hear me clear my throat or notice that I wasn't speaking to her? Why didn't she notice the expression of irritation on my face?*

A few days later when we were talking calmly, I said,

"I've really been wondering about something, but I hesitate asking you this question. I was really intrigued the other day, and I wonder if I could ask you a personal question?" By now I had aroused her curiosity.

"Sure," she said.

"You know last Saturday when I was watching the football game and you made sandwiches for all the kids? Could I ask you why you didn't make one for me?"

"Are you serious?" she asked. She looked at me with such amazement that it really confused me.

"Sure, I'm serious. I would think that since I'm the one who earns all the money for food around here that you would have made me something to eat too."

"You know, I really can't believe that you would even ask a question like that," she said. By now, I was thinking, *Maybe I shouldn't have asked. Maybe I should know the answer.* It seemed very obvious to her, but it didn't seem obvious to me at all.

"Norma, I really don't see it. I admit I am blind in some areas," I pursued, "and I can see this is one of them. Would you mind telling me?"

"Sometimes women are accused of being stupid, but we aren't," she answered. "We don't just set ourselves up to be criticized." She seemed to think that explained why she hadn't made me a sandwich.

"I can understand that. But what does that have to do with the sandwiches?"

"Do you realize that every time I make you a sandwich, you say something critical about it? 'Norma, you didn't give me enough lettuce . . . Is this avocado ripe? You put too much mayonnaise on this. Hey, how about some butter? Well, it's a little dry'. . . .

"Maybe you've never realized it, but you have had a critical statement for every sandwich I ever made. I just wasn't up to being criticized the other day. It wasn't worth it. I don't enjoy being criticized."

I had egg all over my face because I could recall many times when I had criticized her as she handed me sandwiches. But "every" time? I wanted to say, "Come on, Norma, let's get realistic! Every time?" But instead I remembered that for a woman, "always" and "never" don't mean the same thing as they do to a man when they're spoken with emotion. Norma's tone of voice and facial expression as well as her words were telling me this was something that really bothered her. I was simply eating the fruit of my ways. I sowed criticism and reaped an empty plate. I am happy to say that after that experience I began praising every sandwich she made for me, and now she unhesitantly makes them for me.

Shortly after Marilyn left Bob, I asked her if she could recall things for which Bob had praised her. She couldn't remember a single time during their twenty-plus years of marriage. Her children confirmed it. They agreed that their mother had never served a single dinner that their father didn't criticize in at least one way. He had complained when the salt and pepper weren't on the table or when she didn't cook the meat just right. She finally reached the point where she didn't even want to be near his critical personality. She left him for another man.

"I'm kind of happy she's leaving me, because she never wants to do anything with me anyway," Bob said. "She's a party-pooper and a loner. She excludes me from her activities. Do you know she never wanted to go on a vacation with me? I've tried and I've tried, but she never wants to. I'm disgusted with her too."

We didn't discuss his marital problems until after he told me about his job change due to friction with his former boss.

"How did he treat you, Bob?" I asked.

"He'd come out to the shop where I was the foreman, and he'd look for one little thing to yell at me about in front of all my men. That really hurt me deeply. Then he would go back to his office, and I'd continue working my fingers to the bone. He'd never notice how hard I worked or even say anything positive about it. I couldn't take it any more, so I asked for a transfer."

I asked Bob, "Would you take a vacation with your boss?"

"Are you kidding? That would be the worst thing in the world," he answered.

"How about doing other activities with him?"

"No way! He's so critical he'd even ruin a trip to Hawaii!"

What I told Bob next blew open his mind to finally understand his wife. I pointed out how as a husband he was just like his boss, and his face dropped and tears came to his eyes.

"You're right. No wonder Marilyn never wanted to go anywhere with me. I never think about things she does to please me, and I'm always criticizing her in front of the children and our friends."

But it was too late. Marilyn was already in love with another man. Though Bob changed drastically and is now much more sensitive to women, his wife divorced him and remarried.

Women need praise. We should be able to understand their need because we, too, want to know that we are of value to other people. One of the ways we know we're needed is when others express appreciation for *who we are* and *what we do*.

The Scriptures remind us that our major relationships involve praise:

1. Praising God (Ps. 100:4).
2. Praising our wives (Prov. 31:28).
3. Praising others; for example, our Christian friends (Eph. 4:29).

I can vividly remember my boss saying years ago, "If only I had ten men like you, we could change the world." After that, I was so motivated I couldn't do enough for him.

Teachers know how praise motivates children. One teacher said she praised each student in her third-grade class every day, without exception. Her students were the most motivated, encouraged, and enthusiastic in the school. When my substitute high school geometry teacher praised me regularly, my "D" average climbed to an "A" in six weeks.

Knowing how significant praise can be, why do we as husbands fail to express it to our wives? Several reasons. The most common is preoccupation with our own needs, vocation, and activities. We lose sight of the positive and helpful qualities in our wives when we are preoccupied. Even worse, we fail to acknowledge our wives' helpful traits when we do notice them.

When a husband forgets his wife's need for praise, the marriage is usually on its way downhill. And if he constantly expresses the bitter instead of the sweet, his marriage will become less fulfilling every day. Criticism is devastating, especially when voiced in anger or harshness (Prov. 15:1, 4). When a husband rails against his wife for her unique feminine qualities, he conveys a lack of approval for her as a person. This automatically weakens their relationship.

Charlie Jones, in the book *Life Is Tremendous*, says we really can't enjoy life until we learn how to see and say something positive about everything. Though *none of us will ever be completely positive* about life, he says, we can be *in the process* of learning, growing, and developing toward a positive attitude.

If you develop a positive attitude, not only will others want to be around you more often, but your wife will also benefit tremendously. She will have a greater sense of worth and value, knowing you have provided the encouragement only a husband can give.

Encourage your wife and deepen your marriage relationship by following these two simple steps in learning how to praise her.

PRAISE HER (AT LEAST) ONCE A DAY

Promise yourself to tell your wife daily what you appreciate about her. Promise yourself—not her—because she might develop expectations and be hurt if you forget. Begin by learning to verbalize your thoughts of appreciation.

Here are some typical statements wives have told me they enjoy hearing:

1. "What a meal! The way you topped that casserole with sour cream and cheese. . . . M-m-m-m . . . that was delicious."
2. (This next one is great with an early-morning kiss.) "Honey, I sure love you. You're special to me."
3. While in the company of friends say, "This is *my* wife. She's the greatest!"
4. Put little notes on the refrigerator like, "I loved the way you looked last night."
5. "You're such a dedicated wife to make my lunch every day."

6. "Our kids are really blessed to have a mother like you. You take such good care of them."
7. "I don't know if I prefer the dress or what's in it better."
8. "Do I like your hairstyle? I'd like any hairstyle you have just because it's on you."
9. "I'd love to take you out tonight just to show you off."
10. "Honey, you've worked so hard. Why don't you sit down and rest for a while before dinner? I can wait."
11. "You're so special to me that I'd like to do something special for you right now. Why don't you take a bubble bath and relax. I'll do up the dishes and get the kids started on their homework."

In her book *Forever My Love*, Margaret Hardisty emphasized that women tend to approach life on an emotional plane while men approach it on a more logical, sometimes coldly objective one. Therefore, when you praise your wife, it's important to use words and actions that communicate praise *from her point of view*. Anything that is romantic or deals with building deeper relationships usually pleases wives.

BE CREATIVE WITH YOUR PRAISE

One husband won his wife back partly through creative praise. He bought 365 pieces of wrapped candy, wrote a special message on every wrapper, and then sealed them again. She opened one piece every day and read what he appreciated about her for a full year.

A woman loves to find hidden notes—in her jewelry box, the silver drawer, the medicine cabinet. . . . Search for ways to praise your wife. The possibilities are endless.

What kind of praise would you like to hear from your boss? Try a little of it on your wife. You may say, "Well, I don't need too much praise. I'm secure in my job, and I really don't need it." Then interview some of those who work with you to see how they would appreciate being praised. Some of their ideas might work with your wife. Also, ask your wife what kind of praise she likes to hear.

DON'T DRAW ATTENTION TO HER UNATTRACTIVE FEATURES

Wrinkles, gray hair, and excess weight are definitely not on the list of possible conversation starters. Even your casual comments about them can make your wife insecure—she may fear being traded in on a "newer model." She knows divorce is just too easy and common nowadays.

One husband wrote his wife a cute poem about how much he loved her little wrinkles and how he loved caressing her "cellulose cells." His card, though softened with flowers, made her cry for hours. Men, we have to praise our wives without drawing attention to what they believe are their unattractive features.

That doesn't mean you should use insincere flattery. Have you ever been to a party where someone compliments you and you know inside he or she don't mean what they say? Sometimes a husband will casually remark, "Oh, yeah, I really like that dress." But his wife can generally detect his insincerity. Even if you don't like her dress, you can say something sincere like, "Honey, the dress isn't half as good-looking as you are."

Did you know you can even find something to praise in your wife's faults? The chart *How to Find the Positive Side to Your Wife's "Negative" Traits* can get you started on finding the positive aspects in the things you consider her "flaws."

HOW TO FIND THE POSITIVE SIDE TO YOUR WIFE'S "NEGATIVE" TRAITS

Negative	Positive
1. Nosy	She may be very *alert* or *sociable*.
2. Touchy	She may be very *sensitive*.
3. Manipulating	She may be a very *resourceful* person with many creative ideas.
4. Stingy	She may be very *thrifty*.
5. Talkative	She may be very *expressive* and *dramatic*.
6. Flighty	She may be an *enthusiastic* person with *cheerful vitality*.
7. Too serious	She may be a very *sincere* and *earnest* person with *strong convictions*.
8. Too bold	She may have *strong convictions*, *uncompromising* with her own standards.
9. Rigid	She may be a *well-disciplined* person with *strong convictions*.
10. Overbearing	She may be a very *confident* person—sure of herself.
11. A dreamer	She may be very *creative* and *imaginative*.
12. Too fussy	She may be very *organized* and *efficient*.

Specific praise is far better than *general* praise. For example, "That was a great dinner" doesn't do nearly as much for her as, "The asparagus with the nutmeg sauce was fantastic. I've never had asparagus that tasted so good. I don't know how you can take plain, ordinary vegetables and turn them into such mouth-watering delights."

"You're a great mom" won't send her into orbit, but this might: "I'm really grateful that I married a woman who is so sensitive that she knows just the perfect way of making our kids feel important. They're sure lucky to have such a sensitive mother."

There is no right or wrong time to praise your wife. She'll love it when you're alone or when you're with the children and friends. Make sure you don't limit your praise to public or private times. If you only praise her in public, she might suspect you're showing off for your friends. If you only praise her in private, she may feel you're embarrassed about doing it.

Whenever you praise her, it's important that your full attention be on her. If she senses that your mind or feelings are elsewhere, your praise will be less meaningful to her.

As you learn how to praise your wife genuinely and consistently, you'll begin to see a new sparkle in her eyes and new life in your relationship.

HOW TO TALK ABOUT PRAISE WITH YOUR WIFE

1. *Learn to "prime the pump."*

Husband What kind of praise do you really enjoy receiving from people?
Wife Oh I don't know. As long as it's sincere, I'll like it.
Husband Do you feel I praise you enough?
Wife I think so.
Husband (priming the pump) How about last week's meals? Would you appreciate it if I let you know more often how much I enjoy your cooking?
Wife Oh, yes, I remember I went to a lot of extra effort on two meals last week, and you didn't even mention it. . . .

Now you've got the water flowing. If you can take it, keep pumping. Show your *concern* and *understanding* by saying things like, "That must really hurt you when I don't say anything. You deserve a medal for putting up with me." Comfort her and let her get rid of some of her pent-up feelings.

2. Look for the hidden meaning behind her words.

Husband	Dear, remember last week when I thanked you for the meal? Did I overdo it in front of Steve and Mary?
Wife	Don't worry about it—it's okay.
Husband	Even when I said, "I'm glad we had company over; she's never cooked better"?
Wife	Oh, yeah, I did feel bad. You made it sound like I don't cook good meals for you unless we have company.
Husband	I thought you might have felt bad. Let's see, what would have been a better way to say what I meant?

A husband needs to help his wife be as honest and straightforward as possible so he can know where the relationship is strained. So many times during our early married years I asked Norma not to "beat around the bush" or "play games with me." I needed the facts in order to adjust my behavior and learn how to be a better husband. I hope you encourage your wife to be as straightforward as possible to help build a deeper, more fulfilling relationship.

FOR PERSONAL REFLECTION

1. How do we develop a general positive attitude? 1 Thessalonians 5:16–18; Romans 8:28; James 1:2–3; Hebrews 12:11, 15.
2. What does praising God show us about our relationship with Him? Psalm 100:4.

7

What Women Admire Most About Men

"Reprove a wise man, and he will love you."

Proverbs 9:8

"I'm quitting on Monday," Jim yelled as he blasted through the front door. Elaine greeted him quietly and listened to her husband's outburst of anger. "My boss finally did it! I'm not working for him any more," he said. Giving him time and her full attention, Elaine let Jim vent his frustration. Then when he had poured it all out, she began to help him rethink the situation. She reminded him that he could never replace the ideal working conditions or the six-figure income. Soon Jim had changed his mind. Since then, he has told me it was the best decision he ever made. Today he enjoys his job more than ever.

When Jim *honored* Elaine's advice—when he gave high value to her input—he not only made a wise vocational decision but also a wise marital decision. Her respect and admiration for him greatly increased in response to his openness.

The proverb that honor follows humility is still true today (Prov. 15:33). And even more significant is the truth that the man who regards reproof *will* be honored (Prov. 13:18).

121

IF ONLY

Humility is an inner attitude which is evidenced by an openness to the ideas and suggestions of others. It is the recognition that we are not all-knowing, that we can make mistakes, that we can always gain more knowledge and understanding.

The inability to accept advice from others can destroy a relationship. Read how Larry had to learn the hard way to take his wife's correction seriously.

Lynn had tried for ten years to explain to Larry how badly he made her feel, but Larry simply couldn't understand. His first problem was preferring his relatives over his wife. Whenever he and Lynn were around his family, he expected her to change her schedule to fit in with his family's. It didn't matter what she had planned. To make matters worse, Larry always took their side and defended them during arguments.

Larry also had a habit of making more commitments than he was able to fulfill—a promise here and a promise there. He was often guilty of forgetting his commitments. He didn't mean any harm. In fact, his intentions were good. He wanted so much to make people happy that he couldn't say no when asked to do something.

Year after year, Lynn tried to think of creative ways to point out these two problems to Larry, but nothing seemed to get through to him. Finally during one particularly straining visit to their hometown, Lynn broke down and cried. She openly expressed dislike for his relatives, bringing on Larry's lectures and retaliation. Neither of them could handle the emotional scene, so Larry drove the car to a parking lot. He sat there for nearly an hour, trying to understand the problem, but he simply couldn't. Larry and Lynn tried to discuss their problem once again as they began the long drive home. Lynn finally hit just the right combination of words that made sense to Larry.

"Oh, so that's why you don't like my relatives," he said. "Now I see why you don't want to move back to our hometown. When we're with my relatives, I always choose their feelings over yours. You feel second-rate. That makes sense now." Lynn was thrilled. One problem down, one to go.

But Larry remained just as blind to the second problem as he had been to the first. Though Lynn tried to tell him, he finally had to learn it from his friends through a very painful experience. Six of his buddies called a special meeting to tell him about his problem with over-commitment. They had all suffered from his neglect. Graphically, yet lovingly, they explained to Larry that his inability to say no was causing them to be resentful toward him. Larry was straining his friendship with each of them. He was so embarrassed and humiliated by this two-hour meeting that his first thought was, *Why didn't I listen to Lynn?*

His wife was relieved to see that he finally understood his second major problem. Her respect for him automatically increased because of his willingness to improve once he finally comprehended his faults. He became eager to expend the effort and study necessary to learn how to love Lynn (and others) properly.

Let's set some goals: that we as husbands decide to be wise and open ourselves to correction (Prov. 9:8–9). That we be willing to listen to the lessons in each chapter of this book, however painful or difficult, and with our new knowledge commit ourselves to building a better marriage. A better marriage doesn't just happen. It takes serious effort channeled in the right direction. The basic principles presented in each chapter, taken one at a time, will *correct or prevent* the most serious pitfalls we face in marriage.

Some of us entered marriage with an extremely limited knowledge of how to develop a fulfilling relationship with our wives. But it's not hopeless. With a great deal of teaching and patience on their part, *we can learn*. A man needs to take an honest inventory to *assess* where he is in his marriage and be able to *admit* that he might have a long way to go. Your wife can certainly help with that inventory and suggested corrections.

IF I'M OPEN TO MY WIFE'S CORRECTION, DO I GIVE UP BEING THE LEADER?

A man may resist being open to correction from his wife because he feels it somehow negates his position as the leader of the home. If he listens to his wife's complaints or suggestions to improve their relationship and acts on them, he fears it means letting his wife make every decision or giving up control of the home.

I've noticed that almost without exception, the same man who has so much difficulty accepting correction from his wife, also struggles with accepting correction from others. Not only that, but he is usually an expert at criticizing his spouse for her many faults.

Without question, the Scriptures call the man to be the leader and head of the home. Yet like Christ, we are to lead in love—and love does not exist apart from discipline and correction. The Bible tells us that everyone whom the Lord loves, He corrects. I've found that God often uses a man's wife to point out areas in relationships he needs to grow in—correction that can actually help him to love his family and even God in a deeper, more meaningful way.

Although a man may fear that responding to suggestions from his wife might "open the flood gates" to her trying to take over the marriage, I have seen just the opposite to be true. When a woman sees her husband's willingness to accept correction—a mark of someone who wants to gain wisdom—she is more willing to follow his leadership in the home because she values him more highly.

HOW WOULD YOU DESCRIBE THE IDEAL WIFE?

Can you imagine the ecstatic feeling you would have if your wife volunteered the question, "How can I become a better wife?" The honor you would feel would be overwhelming. Of course, it would be absurd to expect this kind of question to come up between most husbands and wives. But just close your eyes for a moment, lean back in your chair, and picture your wife asking you such a question. It would be great, wouldn't it?

If you want your wife to do this for you, first set the example and work on becoming a better husband. *Ask her how you can improve as a husband.*

You'll give her new hope for gaining the type of marriage she's always wanted. If she sees you are sincere, ultimately she'll become far more responsive to your needs and desires.

Do you want to be the type of husband wives complain about the most? All you need is an arrogant, all-knowing attitude and an unwillingness to admit when you're wrong. Three words produced such disgust in one wife that she said, "I get sick inside and ask myself, 'Why did I ever marry this man? What a mess I have gotten myself into.'" What were those three words? "*I'll never change.*" According to Scripture, that's a very foolish statement (Prov. 12:15; 18:2).

"*I'll never change,*" her husband repeated, "so don't try

to change me and don't tell me where I need to change. If you think changing is so important, then why don't *you* change and just leave me alone. The biggest change our marriage needs is for you to keep your mouth shut!"

Wives tell me they admire and honor a husband who admits when he is wrong, especially when he openly seeks his wife's advice on how to improve. I believe a man needs to *motivate himself* to become more interested in his wife's ideas on how he can improve (Prov. 9:9). Then when he has asked her advice, he should observe the following:

LISTEN TO WHAT SHE'S REALLY SAYING

Look for the meaning behind your wife's statements. It is easier to avoid reacting solely to her words if you actively search for the meaning behind them. Have you ever said to your wife, "You're wrong. I don't *always* do that. Don't you think you're exaggerating?" She probably didn't mean *always*, as in "every single time." That's just her way to emphasize a point. The *wise* husband looks beyond that offensive word and says, "Tell me how you're feeling right now. Tell me some of the thoughts behind what you just said. Tell me why you feel you need to use the word 'always.'" Reassure her that she does not have to explain in detail right away. Ask if she'd like to think about it for a day or two. A genuine learner does not put demands on others, forcing them to comply with his impatient desires immediately. He gives others time to feel, think, and change their words.

Many a husband has refused to listen to his wife's correction because of hang-ups over her choice of words. Words have no meaning apart from the interpretation we each place upon them. It is our responsibility in communicating with our wives to understand their *true* intentions.

A husband's tone of voice and facial expressions will reveal whether he has a sincere motivation to learn. His wife will not be as honest if she perceives that he is not really serious about learning and changing.

Chapter 10 delves more into deep communication, so I will conclude with this summary: *Avoid reacting to the words your wife uses and look for the meaning or intention behind them.*

LET HER WORDS SINK IN

Let your wife's advice sink in like a good spring rain. Hold off on responding until you have deeply received what she has said. Norma told me for years that I frowned when I said certain things to our children. She told me they felt I was angry with them, that I was rejecting them. My furrowed brow frightened them, she said. "I'm not frowning, and I'm not angry," I told her. But after I *took the time* to look in the mirror, I said, "You're right. I need to work on that. I appreciate your sharing that with me."

HOLD YOURSELF ACCOUNTABLE
FOR FAILURE

When my children were very young, I used to flick them with my finger on their foreheads or arms when they misbehaved. If one of them was chewing food with his mouth open, I would reach across the table and flick him on the head and say, "Cut that out." Norma has made me aware of how this belittles and wounds our children. What a degrading action! Besides, it must hurt. It even hurts my finger.

I knew deep inside that flicking them was not right. Sometimes, right when I did it, Norma would ask, "Kari, how does that make you feel?"

Kari replied, "It always makes me feel bad when dad does it."

I finally came up with a way to break myself of this habit. I said to each of the children, "If I flick you on the head in anger or irritation, then I will pay you a dollar for each time I do it." (I thought this might work well because I don't like to give money away.) Believe me, my kids are alert enough not to let any slip by. And it's been a long time since I've flicked one of them.

Eventually, you can sometimes even laugh together about something that used to be a problem. On one occasion my son Greg came into the house eating a delicious-looking chocolate candy bar he had just bought. I asked him for a bite. *It was good.* Then Kari and Michael came in and wanted a bite too. Greg soon wished he hadn't unwrapped his candy in front of us. Little Michael didn't think Greg was too generous with the portions he doled out, so he decided to buy his own. He asked Greg where he bought it and how much it cost. Then with a longing look in his eyes, he said, "Dad, would you please flick me? I need a dollar."

SEEK HER FORGIVENESS

As I said before, a woman won't set herself up to be hurt. If you have offended her in the past, she won't be eager to share advice or correction in the present. Seek her forgiveness to reestablish the spirit of communication. Her admiration and respect for you will be strengthened and maintained by your willingness to admit your wrongs. Since chapter 5 dealt with forgiveness, review it from time to time when you need more help in this area.

RECEIVE HER ADVICE WITH GRATEFULNESS

Oh, the bounty of a grateful man—less nagging, more admiration and gentleness from his wife. When a man shows genuine gratefulness for his wife's correction, she feels a greater freedom to be more gentle the next time she corrects him. No need to nag when you have a grateful listener. A wife also admires her husband more when he is willing to thank her for her advice or correction. (The only exception is when a wife has been *deeply* hurt by her husband. Then she needs his time and patience until she is able to respond with admiration and gentleness. Don't quit trying when you're so close to success.)

Continue to look for the meaning behind what your wife says, let it sink in, and establish consequences for your failure. When you continue to thank her for helping you, you will begin to see the development of a stronger relationship.

Though the following illustration is the story of a father and son, it can be applied to a husband and wife. Jim's dad was irresponsible in many ways during his son's formative childhood and teen years. He disciplined Jim by kicking him, ridiculing him, scolding him, and slapping him. As a result, his son withdrew in spirit and, consequently, his mind and emotions also withdrew. He moved out of the house. When I explained to this father how he had crushed his son in the past, he realized he had not only damaged *their* relationship but possibly his son's future relationships.

Because he really wanted to have his son back emotionally, mentally, and physically, this father made an appointment to see his son. It took a lot of nerve, but he admitted to Jim that he was wrong and was sorry for not being the kind of father he should have been. During his confession, he mentioned all the hurtful incidents he could recall.

His son remembered these specific incidents too. "But, dad, that's not all." Then for the next few minutes he reminded his father of all the other things he had done to hurt him. Jim's father was amazed that his son still remembered it all so vividly. They wiped the slate clean. And for the first time Jim reached out to hug his dad.

When you offend your wife, she withdraws mentally, emotionally, and physically. But you can learn to draw her back. Just your willingness to learn will encourage her to respond as she becomes secure in the knowledge that you really want to change.

FOR PERSONAL REFLECTION

1. How can a husband become a wise man and increase his love for his wife? Proverbs 9:8–9.
2. What are the consequences of not listening or listening to God's reproofs? Proverbs 1:22–33.

8

If Your Wife's Not Protected, You Get Neglected

> "For no one ever hated his own flesh, but nourishes and cherishes it, just as Christ also does the church (emphasis mine)."
>
> Ephesians 5:29

Dan and Janet had been married more than twenty years when he called me in a panic. "Janet's leaving me for another man," he said. He was crushed and bewildered. "Gary, is there anything you can do to help me?"

Dan's main problem was easily detectable when we met to talk. Let me explain why he lost her by using his hobby as an illustration.

Dan was an avid, meticulous, and knowledgeable gardener. Lush flower gardens defined the borders of his well-kept yard. Pruned trees shaded the delicate greenery from the hot summer sun. Dan knew where to plant each variety of flower so it would obtain the proper sunlight and soil. Since each plant had special needs, Dan had taken the time to research those needs so he would know exactly how much fertilizer and other nutrients they required. The results were magnificent. But while his garden was a glorious blaze of harmony in nature, his marriage was wilting from lack of *paper work*

attention. He entered his work and other activities with the same enthusiasm he applied to gardening, which left little time for Janet.

Dan hadn't the faintest idea what Janet's needs were. He had very little knowledge about how to protect her from the "scorching summer sun and wind." Not only did he fail to protect her, but he convinced her through his logical arguments that she should handle household responsibilities that she had said were too much for her. Throughout their twenty years together Dan had failed to listen to her many, many pleadings for tender protection.

Janet was not only holding down a full-time job, but was also responsible for keeping the finances, cooking the meals, cleaning the house, and training the children. She faced many crises alone while Dan was fishing, hunting, or cultivating his posies. He could not recognize Janet's need to have a strong and gentle man to support her during times of stress, one who would protect her from some of the "dirty work" (we all need protection like this at times). She needed to be accepted and loved as a person with her own special physical limitations. When Dan repeatedly failed her, she looked elsewhere.

When a man doesn't understand his wife's limitations or explains them away as laziness, numerous misunderstandings can result. For example, a woman with several small children can be totally exhausted both physically and mentally by five in the afternoon. If her husband doesn't recognize this, he may resent her avoidance of sexual relations at ten or eleven at night when she is genuinely too tired to even think of a romantic experience with him.

Some men think that their wives will take advantage of them if they are gentle, loving, and giving. Keith was willing to gamble money to see if his wife would take advantage of him. He took his wife to a shopping center for her birthday. He told her he would like to help her buy some clothes but never mentioned the amount she could spend. Two hours and ten shops later, as his feet began to ache, Keith wondered whether this birthday outing was a good idea or not.

"Mary, how do you like this dress? It would look good on you."

"No, I don't like it."

Finally they wandered into a nice shop where Mary found a coordinated skirt, jacket, blouse, and pantsuit that she liked well enough to buy. Though the money was beginning to add up, Keith said, "Mary, look at this. Here's a dress on sale."

Mary liked the dress and tried it on.

Keith said, "Why don't you get it?"

"Keith, I shouldn't be spending any more of our money."

"Oh, no, go ahead and get it," Keith replied. "I like it. Hey, Mary, what do you think of this dress?"

"This is getting ridiculous," Mary protested. But she tried it on when Keith insisted.

At this point, he was beginning to wonder if she would buy every dress that he told her to buy. "Oh, I like this one, Mary."

"Keith, I cannot buy another dress," she said. "This is getting ridiculous. We can't afford all this."

"Ah, what difference does it make?" he asked. "You're more important than money, and even if I have to work extra, I'm happy to do it." He really put the pressure on her to buy the dress.

She replied, "I'm embarrassed. I can't buy another dress. Please let's pay for these and go get something to eat."

"Come on, Mary. Would you buy just one more for me? I just want this to be a very special day for you!"

"Keith, I can't do it," she said.

"Okay, we'll pay for them. I want you to be happy and satisfied."

Keith didn't admit until some time later that he just wanted to prove that a woman well-treated will not take advantage. He praised her for her thriftiness and caution, proud of her willingness to work with him for the financial security they both desired. Now he never worries that Mary will overspend because he knows she will look for the right price and the best buy. This experience has also convinced him that Mary will not take advantage of him in other areas of their life.

I'm not advocating that you try this with your wife or in any way "test" or manipulate her. However, I have often seen what happens when a husband learns what Keith learned: When a wife is treated with tenderness and genuine love, she won't take advantage of the situation.

When the Scripture teaches that a husband is to *cherish* his wife (Eph. 5:29), it basically means to protect her, especially in the areas that cause her emotional or physical discomfort.

THREE WAYS TO PROTECT YOUR WIFE AND HELP HER BECOME MORE FULFILLED

1. *Discover where your wife needs protection.*

First, a husband needs to discover areas in which his wife feels vulnerable. Through informal discussions and observation on your part, you can compile mental lists of the major and minor areas where she is frustrated or fearful. Driving a car is one of my wife's vulnerable areas. Because she was involved in a serious auto accident in which some good friends were killed, she is naturally very alert to any possible danger when she is driving or even riding in a car.

It would only frustrate her if I did not give her the freedom to be cautious, knowing her past circumstances. She also feels vulnerable when driving long distances alone in the winter because she fears the car will break down. When we lived in Chicago, the car broke down twice, and she had to accept help from passing motorists. Both she and the children could conceivably have been hurt or abused. Since I am aware of her fear, I don't push her to drive long distances alone any more.

What about her physical limits?

Many times a man treats his wife too roughly. He is unaware that his wife's physical make-up keeps her from enjoying roughness even when being playful.

One wife told me that her husband enjoyed wrestling but didn't realize how much it had injured her in the past. He never intentionally hurt her, but she would find bruises on her arms or her body after they had wrestled on the carpet. He was rough with her in other ways too. For example, one night they were in the grocery store, and she lingered a while in the book section. Her husband was waiting for her in the parking lot with a sack of dog food and other items. When she caught up with him, he said, "No wonder you didn't hurry out here. You're not the one holding all the groceries."

"Well, all right, I'll help you," she said. He playfully threw the sack of dog food at her, hitting her in the stomach so forcefully that it left her gasping for breath. The ride home was silent. As they pulled up in the driveway, he said, "The reason I was quiet wasn't because I was mad at you. I was mad at myself for hurting you again." He wanted to make an effort to change his behavior because he realized she needed to be treated with more tenderness and more carefulness.

What about financial pressures?

A man also needs to protect his wife from unnecessary financial stress. Many wives endure a tremendous amount of pressure because of a husband's irresponsibility with finances. To compensate for overspending, a husband may force his mate to work when she would rather be home with the children. In fact, some husbands demand it, feeling "she should do her part." If a woman is home all day, her husband may expect her to handle bill payments and financial bookkeeping for the family because he wonders what she does all day anyway. He might think, *I work eight hours every day. The least she can do is pay the bills.*

If it were just a matter of bookkeeping, this would not be a problem. But when it comes to facing angry bill collectors, juggling figures in a checkbook that won't balance, coping with mounting pressures resulting from insufficient money, deciding which bill to pay first, and making phone calls to appease businesses, the burden *can* become physically and emotionally too much for some wives. The problem is magnified if the husband appears to be spending money loosely and enjoying himself.

I made this mistake in the early years of our marriage. Norma worked for a bank, and I logically concluded that anyone working for a bank would obviously be able to take care of the money at home. Since financial matters were a weak point for me at that time, I asked her if she would take that responsibility, which she graciously did for four or five years. One day, though, she came to me in tears, laid the records, the checkbook, and all the bills in my lap and said that she just couldn't handle it any more. You see, we had two checkbooks between us and only one checking account. I would write a check, hoping the money was in the bank. It was a tremendous pressure on my wife. Today

I am very grateful she handed over that responsibility, because it forced me to take more responsibility for the financial well-being of our family.

What about expecting her to do all the cooking?

So many men treat their wives as objects to be used. They don't verbalize it, but they maintain the inward conviction that women should remain in the kitchen cooking or cleaning while they play golf, hunt, or watch the game on TV. Have you ever noticed during get-togethers with friends or relatives that the women are usually the ones who are expected to work in the kitchen while the men just shoot the breeze? Little girls are trained to watch for the special needs of a male family member. For instance, a mother will say, "Go ask daddy if he wants a glass of iced tea." But we seldom see little boys asked to do the same thing.

I had a real problem with role expectation during our first few years of marriage: it was Norma's job to cook and my responsibility to fix the car. I finally realized that it was okay for me to cook and clean the house, especially if Norma was needing a rest or some time alone away from all of us. We as men need to take a close look at our traditional roles and choose what is best based on genuine love and the commitment to cherish our mates.

Think of your wife's special limitations before expecting her to take on *added* responsibilities. Such forethought will avoid extra strain on your relationship and protect your wife's mental, spiritual, emotional, and physical life.

What about her need for rest?

Why is it that some men feel their wives need less sleep than they do? While the husband sleeps, the wife prepares breakfast and takes care of the children. This is certainly true where babies are involved. During our early years of marriage, when my children would cry during the night, I automatically expected my wife to get up and take care of them. And she did. Never did I feel compelled to get up and take care of the kids. Be tender and alert to her physical needs. Be the leader in taking whatever steps are needed to insure that your wife gets the rest she needs.

What about the pressure of the children?

Often my wife has said how much she appreciates the times I take charge of the kids when I come home from work. I get them out from underfoot so she is able to finish dinner peacefully. She is also grateful for the time to be alone. She likes me to take them outside to play, into another room to read, or just to talk to them about whatever topic they choose. After the meal, the children and I often clear the table and wash the dishes to let Norma have some time off. Instead of resenting her need for my help as I once did, I now look forward to helping her as often as I can.

Thoughtful, creative ideas on your part are worth much more than the time or energy they cost. They strengthen your marriage and lift your wife's spirit.

One night Jim thrilled Debbie when he asked her to let him cook dinner, set the table, and feed the children. He told her he had a gift he would give her if she let him do those things—a bottle of bath oil. While she took a leisurely bath, he took care of the household chores. It was only a small gift; it just took a bit of Jim's time. But to Debbie, it meant that he cared enough to give something extra of himself.

What about the added pressure of moving?

A move from one city to another is a major step for a woman. It requires that her husband be extra sensitive to her limitations. Many times a woman's emotional and physical endurance is depleted just from normal day-to-day routines. A move obviously adds additional stress, even when the move is welcomed.

What can cause her the most stress?

We as husbands need to be aware of the amount of stress our wives face daily. To aid your wife with stress, you must first be aware of the situations that cause her the most anxiety. To help you, we have included a list from the *Holmes-Rahe Stress Test*, which ranks items from the greatest amount of stress to the least amount of stress. The higher it is on the list, the greater the stress it produces. Check to see how much stress you and your wife are facing today. (See Holmes-Rahe Stress Test on page 143.)

If your score is 150 or less, there is a 33% chance that you will be in the hospital within two years. If it is 150–300, the chances are 51%; and 300 and above, 80%. Purpose to protect your wife in all areas where she feels fearful or vulnerable. That's the first way to show her how much you cherish her.

2. *Discover how your wife wants to be fulfilled.*

Another way to cherish your wife is to help her become fulfilled as a person. You can do this by discovering her personal goals in life and helping her reach them if possible. We all love to know that someone is pulling for us, that others are cheering when we reach a goal. It makes a woman feel worthwhile and valuable when her husband takes time to help her achieve a personal goal.

From time to time, my wife and I get together on a date, for breakfast out or just a retreat from home. During that time we list our personal goals. We commit ourselves to help each other fulfill those goals. This book is the result of a goal that my wife and I wanted to reach together. Since she was as excited about it as I was, I knew it was okay with her for me to take several weeks away from my family to work on our goal.

I feel so satisfied, knowing my wife is committed enough to sacrifice for my goals, that I get excited when I think of helping her with her goals. Since I know she wants to maintain her physical health as best she can, we decided she should join a health spa. To see that she has the opportunity to exercise regularly, I am happy to babysit sometimes so she can accomplish her personal goal of good physical health.

Sit down with your wife and ask her to name some goals. She might want to finish college, advance in her vocation, study public speaking, learn to sew, or cook some new exotic meals. Her goals may change as she discovers the real pressure or motives behind them. Maybe she says she wants to go back to school, when all she really wants is a couple of days a week away from the children. By relieving her of some of the pressure, you may help channel her energies in the right direction, helping her to reach her *real* personal goals. I believe it is our responsibility to discover our wives' goals and to understand how they want to fulfill themselves as women. Then we must let them be who they want to be by respecting their unique ambitions.

3. *Discover what personal problems your wife wants to solve.*

My wife would like to share with women how to be fulfilled in the home without outside work. Unfortunately, during our early marriage she became timid when speaking to groups, due to another one of my irresponsibilities. I used to correct her grammar or give suggestions on how to improve her teaching methods in an insensitive way. Whenever I heard her share in front of groups, I always called her attention to anything I thought was less than perfect. Little did I know that my wife's nature was so sensitive that she eventually stopped speaking in front of groups because of my criticism. It took five years of my praise and encouragement to heal the wounds I had thoughtlessly inflicted. She is speaking to groups more and more now, but is still quite nervous when I am in the audience.

Has your wife ever told you emphatically in the morning that she is going to lose weight . . . and that very same evening she's eating donuts? The harmful action you can take is to remind her sarcastically of that early-morning commitment. However, you can comfort her by saying nothing at all or by putting your arm around her to say, "I love you for who you are, not for what you decide to do." She probably feels disappointed enough about her lack of will power. Knowing she is loved *as she is* will probably boost her self-confidence and strengthen her will power.

In summary, a woman loves to build a lasting relationship with a man who cares about her enough to let her lean on him when she needs comfort. She needs a man who will understand her fears and limitations so that he can protect her. She feels important when her husband stands up and defends her in the presence of someone who is criticizing her.

Each person is unique, and the only way you can pinpoint your wife's needs is to discuss them with her. You may want to question her to see if she feels that you are protective or helpful enough in these areas:

The family finances
Raising of the children
Household needs and responsibilities
The future—insurance, a will

Her own employment and the people with whom she works
Her friends and relatives

You should also endeavor to discover how she would like to be fulfilled as a person. Ask her to explain two or three goals she has always wanted to accomplish. Then reevaluate your goals together each year.

FOR PERSONAL REFLECTION

1. Clearly define the word "cherish" as it is used in Ephesians 5:29. Ask your pastor for help, or consult a Bible commentary.
2. How does Paul encourage Christians to treat each other? How do you treat your wife? 1 Thessalonians 5:11, 14.

HOLMES-RAHE STRESS TEST
In the past 12 months, which of these have happened to you?

EVENT	VALUE	SCORE
Death of a spouse	100	____
Divorce	73	____
Marital separation	65	____
Jail term	63	____
Death of a close family member	63	____
Personal injury or illness	53	____
Marriage	50	____
Fired from work	47	____
Marital reconciliation	45	____
Retirement	45	____
Change in family member's health	44	____
Pregnancy	40	____
Sex difficulties	39	____
Addition to family	39	____
Business readjustment	39	____
Change in financial status	38	____
Death of close friend	37	____
Change in number of marital arguments	35	____
Mortgage or loan over $10,000	31	____
Foreclosure of mortgage or loan	30	____
Change in work responsibilities	29	____
Son or daughter leaving home	29	____
Trouble with in-laws	29	____
Outstanding personal achievement	28	____
Spouse begins or starts work	26	____
Starting or finishing school	26	____
Change in living conditions	25	____
Revision of personal habits	24	____
Trouble with boss	23	____
Change in work hours, conditions	20	____
Change in residence	20	____
Change in schools	20	____
Change in recreational habits	19	____
Change in church activities	19	____
Change in social activities	18	____
Mortgage or loan under $10,000	18	____
Change in sleeping habits	16	____
Change in number of family gatherings	15	____
Change in eating habits	15	____

IF ONLY

Christmas season . . . . 13 ____
Vacation . . . . 12 ____
Minor violation of the law . . . . 11 ____

TOTAL . . . . ____

144

9

Arguments...
There's A
Better Way

"For this cause a man shall leave his father and mother, and shall *cleave* to his wife; and the two shall become one flesh (emphasis mine)."

Ephesians 5:31

A simple agreement can eliminate heated arguments between you and your wife. No, it's not a divorce!

It is an agreement that will increase the time you and your mate spend discussing important areas *without* that familiar anger and silence routine; it will also build your wife's self-respect.

When my wife and I stumbled upon this concept during a Fourth of July argument several years ago, both of our fuses were getting short. The fireworks show was dull in comparison. I wanted to vacation in Colorado in July; she wanted to go to Florida in August. Since we didn't agree on separate vacations either, the discussion became hotter and hotter with no end in sight. Sizzling, I compared her attitude to some of the more submissive single women from the office.

"You don't have a calm attitude. Besides that, you're wrong," I said.

"I have never met this 'calm woman' you talk about," she replied angrily. "If you can show me just one, I might consider following her example."

At this point, the accidental brainstorm that has helped us avoid heated discussions for several years came to me. I asked Norma if she would be willing to drop the conversation and try an experiment for just two months. If it worked, we'd use it; if not, we'd search for another solution.

"Will you not make decisions in the home that affect me and the rest of the family without my complete agreement?" I asked her. "And I won't make any decisions affecting you unless I have your full consent."

I didn't know if the experiment would work, but I did know that I was tired of arguments and futile discussions that led nowhere except to tears and angry silence. Since I worked for an organization that taught family harmony, I was desperate to achieve it in my own home. (You've heard of the plumber with leaky pipes, haven't you?)

Many things had to change if we were going to agree to agree. We had to reason together for longer periods of time. We were also forced to discover the reasons behind each other's comments. I had to search for the meaning behind Norma's words and understand her frame of reference if I hoped to convince her of my point of view. Several of our first discussions ended with the consensus that since we couldn't agree we would just wait. Amazingly enough, many "problems" seemed to solve themselves—or at least their importance seemed to diminish as the days passed.

In spite of the success of our agreement, I went back on it after two months. Hearing a growing argument between Kari and Greg at the kitchen table, I rushed in to referee just in time to see Greg shove his full plate across the table, spilling it all over Kari. I was about to take Greg upstairs for a little discipline when Norma said she disagreed.

"Well, our experiment doesn't apply in every situation," I said, stopping in my tracks. "I can't relinquish my responsibility as Greg's father just because you don't agree. I'm sorry. I'll have to overrule you this time."

After Greg and I had our "little talk," Norma greeted me coldly in the kitchen.

"Well, Norma, I had to do what I thought was right," I explained. "I wish we could agree in every situation, but it's not practical."

She replied, "I don't think you took the time to find out the facts."

"I saw all I needed to know."

But I had to admit that I didn't know what Kari had done to provoke Greg. Norma had told Kari to make sandwiches for Greg. Kari probably didn't want to do it in the first place, so when Greg didn't want the sandwiches, she tried to force them on him.

"Mom told me to make you sandwiches and you're gonna eat 'em," she said.

"You're not my boss. I don't have to eat them," Greg retorted. And to make his point, he pushed the sandwiches away. But the table was slicker than he anticipated, and the sandwiches slid into Kari's lap.

I admitted to Greg that I was wrong and apologized. To keep such mistakes from happening in the future, obtain all the legal counsel needed from within the family. After all the facts are presented, the family decides who is guilty. We also set up written "contracts" covering desired behaviors and these have been a tremendous help during our children's teenage years. (See my book, *The Key to Your Child's Heart*, for details of this powerful parenting method.)

Whenever Norma and I do not agree on something that affects the family, I have been amazed at the number of times her decision has been right. I'm not sure whether she has a hot line to heaven or what, but somehow she can sense when something is not right. Committing ourselves to agree has brought more harmony and deeper communication than anything else we practice. It has increased my wife's self-worth and eliminated pressure-packed arguments.

Constant disagreement can only weaken a marriage relationship. That's probably why Paul emphasized having oneness of spirit and mind in the church. He likened the struggle for oneness to an athlete *striving* to reach the goal (Phil. 1:27). Likewise, as husbands and wives we can learn to enter into a oneness or agreement.

As I mentioned earlier, I know some men will react strongly to having their wives share in any of the decisions that affect the family. Like battlefield generals, they demand acceptance of their orders, not input from those people the decisions will most affect.

As we'll discuss at the end of the chapter, there may be rare times of deadlock when you'll have to make the final decision that goes against your wife's or your family's feelings. However, I've found that by my slowing down, talking through major decisions with Norma and the children, and valuing their opinions and input, over the years such impassable situations have been almost nonexistent.

The rest of this chapter discusses the specific consequences of not agreeing on decisions that affect the family and ways to apply the "agreement" principle in your family.

WHAT HAPPENS WHEN YOU MAKE ALL THE DECISIONS

When a wife is left out of the decision-making process, she feels insecure, especially if the decisions involve financial security or living conditions. Her constant state of insecurity spreads like a disease to produce instability in other areas of the marriage.

Steve and Bonney had been struggling to make just enough money to put food on the table. His small business was requiring eighteen hours a day on his part, and she was putting in at least eight hours a day at the office, even though she was seven months pregnant. Steve flew East to show his business ideas to a multimillionaire. The man was impressed and made Steve a generous offer which he accepted in less than five minutes. It was the only "reasonable" course of action.

He could hardly wait to call Bonney and tell her the great news in "logical" order so she could get as excited as he was. He told her, "First, you won't have to work anymore. Second, he's giving me 20 percent of the profits—he says I'll be a millionaire in a year. Third, you won't believe how beautiful it is back here, and he's going to pay all of the moving expenses."

Steve was shocked to hear uncontrollable weeping on the other end of the line. At first he thought she was crying for joy (I know it's hard to believe, but he actually thought that).

As soon as Bonney caught a breath, she had a chance to ask some questions Steve considered totally ridiculous (in fact, he thought her mind had snapped). She asked questions like, "What about our parents?" and "What about our apartment—I just finished the room for the baby." With her third question, Steve, in all of his masculine "sensitivity," abruptly terminated the phone call. She had the nerve to ask if he'd forgotten she was seven months pregnant.

After giving her an hour or two to pull herself together, he called her back. She had gained her composure and agreed to move back east. She left her parents, her friends, her doctor and childbirth classes, and the nursery she had spent so much time preparing for her first child.

It took Bonney almost eight months to adjust to a change that Steve had adjusted to in minutes. Steve never made his million. The business failed eight days before their baby was born, and they moved again. Steve eventually learned his lesson, and today he doesn't make any major change unless Bonney is in agreement. He tries to give her ample time to adjust to other changes as soon as he can foresee them. However, Steve will never forget the loving sacrifices his wife made so many times. He even realizes that questions like "What about our parents?" or "What about the nursery?" can be more meaningful than money.

Husbands can also make their wives feel stupid, inadequate, or like an unnecessary member of the family when they make most of the decisions alone. Many husbands treat their wives as if they don't know anything at all. When a decision comes up in their area of expertise or with regard to financial dealings, their wives might as well forget about participating as far as they are concerned.

Jerry had to lose money before he would respect his wife's judgment. He considered a number of ways to invest some of his earnings, from apartments, to real estate, to the stock market. After talking to developers and reading literature, he decided to buy a lakefront lot in a planned retirement community. He reasoned that if he bought the land during the early development stages, it would be worth quite a bit of money in five to ten years. When Linda found out about his plans, she hesitated to invest their money.

But Jerry thought, *What would she know anyway?* and signed the contract in spite of her objections.

Sometime later when he wanted to sell the land for quick money to invest in a better project, he found it was difficult to sell. Jerry and Linda will probably still have it when they are ready to retire. If Jerry had consulted Linda, not only would he have saved a great deal of money, but he could have given her self-esteem a boost. After all, what's wrong with becoming "one flesh" with our mates? That's God's design!

We husbands would do well to remember that everyone has a different stress-tolerance level. When you ignore your wife in making decisions, you add stress to every area of her life. As I've said before, stress will definitely take its toll by eroding her physical health.

As with so many areas of my marriage, I had to discover this the hard way. As I mentioned earlier, when my work load demanded that I travel a great deal, I didn't ask Norma if she could handle three small children alone; I just assumed she could. As a result of the extra pressure, she came to me on the verge of a physical collapse. I had to take a less responsible position in my company, but I learned the importance of taking care of my family. They bring me much more joy and fulfillment than any job. Today I can enjoy my work more because my family is always beside me. When a man learns to enjoy his family above all else, his activities and his friends take on an even greater meaning as well.

I look back on the past with grief when I think of incidents like the following: Norma and the three children were to pick me up at work at 5:00 P.M. to go for hamburgers. Just as she drove up, I was called to a last-minute staff meeting. I explained quickly that I would join her in a few minutes. Instead, the meeting lasted two hours. I wasn't apologetic, though. I was angry because she had not waited lovingly and patiently for me in the car while appeasing our three hungry children.

If only I could relive that experience! I would say, "Honey, they just called an unexpected meeting. Would you like to go back home and wait for me and feed the children? Then you and I can eat together later." Or I would explain to my associates that I had a previous commitment to my family. Let's face it, not much is usually accomplished at meetings held that late in the day. (And your colleagues' wives might benefit from it, too.)

Finally, arguments are probably the most common side effects of major decisions made apart from any discussion. As anger sharpens the tongue, turning it into a fierce weapon, husbands and wives can end discussions by attacking each other's character. Words spoken during the heat of an argument are sometimes never forgotten. My wife can still remember ugly things I said when we were dating.

If a woman feels threatened during a discussion, she may become angry and demand her way. If her husband doesn't understand that she is acting that way because he threatened her security, he may feel his ego is being attacked or his leadership questioned. And both will pursue the issue like wild dogs, fighting to be the leader of the pack. Instead, each should enter the other's world to achieve mutual understanding.

Suppose a husband who is having difficulties with his wife comes up with the idea of the two of them taking a short vacation for a few days to better their relationship, while leaving the kids with grandma. His wife may say, "You're pressuring me." He feels he has been verbally slapped in the face. He wasn't trying to pressure her, and furthermore, he sees no logical reason *why* she should feel that way. Tempers flare, and argument #1,241 begins. But who's counting? The point is, if a woman says she feels pressured, take her word for it—SHE FEELS PRESSURED! Try to enter her world to discover why she feels that way— don't argue that you didn't intentionally try to pressure her.

If your idea somehow has caused her to say she *feels* pressured, then she *is* pressured.

The chart below gives an example of how to eliminate trivial arguments before they snowball into major flareups.

If she says...	Typical response from a husband	Try this instead...
"You're putting pressure on me."	"I'm not pressuring you. I just wanted to do something so the two of us could be together. Don't accuse me of that."	"Honey, I can sure understand that you're pressured. If you feel what I'm saying is pressuring you, then I can sure accept that. That's not my intent, but I can understand that you feel that way. Can you share at this time any of the reasons why you feel that way?"
"I hate going to the beach. I don't want to go."*	"You used to like the beach before we were married."	"I know I should know why you don't want to go to the beach, but could you tell me just once more some of the reasons why you don't?"
"No, I don't want to go to the ball game with you. I hate those ball games."	"I try to do things with you. The least you could do is to go with me once in a while and support me in something that I enjoy doing."	"Honey, is one of the reasons that you don't like to go because I ignore you so much when I'm at a ball game?"†

---

*She may have several reasons for saying this, one being that she is embarrassed about her figure. At that point a husband needs to be tender, understanding, and gentle. Remember, some women do not feel as relaxed in a bathing suit as a man might.

†If she says yes to that question, ask her for other reasons she resists going to a game. (Remember, if you react negatively to her reasons, she'll be less willing to share her true feelings with you in the future.) You may need to give her "room to breathe" and come back to it all another time. If she says no, ask her to explain why, tenderly and with a real desire to understand her and value her opinion.

HOW TO MAKE DECISIONS TOGETHER

Once you have found a method that works, stick to it. Whenever my wife and I try to take shortcuts, we get into trouble.

After a quick discussion about moving to the country, we located the home of our dreams. I wrote an ad for the paper to sell our home and bought "For Sale" signs to put in the front yard. A neighbor walked across the street to ask how much I was asking for our house. When I quoted the price, he said it was far too low; it might reduce the market value of other houses in the neighborhood.

A vague uneasiness began to gnaw at me. Since Norma and I had not discussed every detail of this upcoming move, I tried to call her but couldn't reach her. I cancelled the ad and plucked the signs out of the yard. When Norma finally arrived home, we filled out the chart we usually use for major decisions and decided, after weighing advantages and disadvantages, that it was not a good idea for us to sell our home at that time.

The simple chart we use helps us reach total agreement on important decisions. We first list all of the reasons, pro and con, for doing something. Second, we list all the reasons, pro and con, for *not* doing it. Third, we evaluate each reason. Will the decision have lasting effects? Is the reason selfish, or will it help others? Finally, we total the pros and cons and see which wins, not *who* wins. Although you may think you have in mind all the reasons you need to make the decision, seeing them ranked in black and white simplifies and streamlines the decision.

The pro-and-con chart forces us as a couple to consider as many facts as possible. For instance, if I am counseling someone, I find I usually cannot help the person until I know plenty of facts about the particular situation. The fewer the facts, the foggier a situation appears. But the more facts I have, the clearer the picture and the easier the solution. If I ask a person to write down all the facts on a piece of paper, often he or she can come up with the solution on his or her own.

Let me give you an example of how the chart works for my family.

A Major Decision—Should I Change Jobs?

This move would mean moving a thousand miles and would involve a cut in pay.

1. List all the reasons, pro and con, for changing jobs and moving my family a thousand miles. (I'll only put down a few of the reasons we used, for purposes of illustration.)

If We Move

What we will gain (pro)
1. We will be able to raise our family in a smaller town.
2. We will gain a greater opportunity to help families in a concentrated way.
3. There are many more camping spots where we're moving, and the weather is warmer year-round.
4. Two of our best friends live in that town.

What we will lose (con)
1. We will be taking a cut in pay. Could we adjust to that?
2. Do we really want to live in a small town and lose all the conveniences of a major city with nice shopping centers?
3. We'll have to move away from our friends whom we love so much.
4. Can we afford to buy our own home?
5. There's not a major airport for convenient travel to my Family Workshops.

2. List all of the reasons, pro and con, for *not* moving my family to a new location and a new job.

If We Stay

What we will gain (pro)
1. We will maintain our present salary.
2. Our children will be educated at a private school.
3. We will continue to use all the shops and stores that we know so well.
4. We will continue all the contacts we have for buying various items at discount.

What we will lose (con)
1. We will lose our opportunity to help families on a personal and consistent basis.
2. We will lose the opportunity for our children to live in a warmer climate with a greater opportunity for involvement in sports and activities.
3. We'll lose our chance to join a church that we as a family really enjoy attending together.
4. We will lose our opportunity as husband and wife to work on our life goals together.

It's important to list reasons for *doing* something and *not doing* something. It forces us to think of different aspects of both viewpoints.

3. Evaluate each of the reasons given in #1 and #2. Make your decision based on your evaluations of #1 and #2.

"Vote YES on the Big Move," Kari's sign read. She had plastered signs all over the house to gain votes in favor of our move to another state. Like a campaign manager, she actively tried to get our other two children to cast their votes for her side.

When voting day came, I passed out a ballot to each family member. The suspense mounted as I read each vote aloud until finally the votes were tallied. "Yes" won unanimously.

The doctrine of majority rule doesn't apply here. If one member had voted "No," I believe it would have been important to consider *why* that member had voted differently. An essential ingredient in making a happy family is total agreement. Discussion should stay open until everyone can agree when possible. Creative alternatives can be considered when it looks as though one member is going to "hang the jury."

What to do if husband and wife are deadlocked on an important decision.

Instead of looking for a referee for the ensuing battle, they should postpone the decision as long as possible in order to gather additional facts. If it comes down to the "wire," they need to decide what is best for the family, and if they still can't agree biblically, he should make his decision with the *family's* best interest in mind. A loving, understanding attitude can melt a wife's heart and give her the security she so desperately wants in times of difficult decisions, even if it takes time to adjust to a decision.

FOR PERSONAL REFLECTION

1. Is a husband instructed to submit to his wife (Eph. 5:21)?
2. What do the verses before and after Ephesians 5:22 mean, where a wife is instructed to submit? Also check Colossians 3:17–19.
3. Since a husband is to love his wife as Christ loves the church, it is essential that we know how Christ loves. What can we learn about Him from Matthew 20:25–28?
4. Write out a simple definition of submission. Consider Romans 12:10.

10

A Successful Marriage...
It's Easier
Than You Think

"While I was with them, I was keeping them in Thy name
which Thou hast given Me; and I guarded them."
John 17:12

When I was newly married, I often asked other couples if
they could tell me the secrets of a happy marriage. They
would usually say, "You and your wife will have problems,
but if it's meant to be, you'll stay together. If not, you'll
separate." Later, when I worried about staying close to my
children, people would answer, "Your teenagers will rebel.
It's just normal."

These philosophies seemed so pessimistic that I became
discouraged whenever our domestic harmony was threatened during an argument. I couldn't find any articles or
books written on how to become a warm, loving family.

However, today I can say without reservation that my
wife is my best friend. This has come about because we
have practiced a principle learned from several successful
families. Practicing this principle also has eliminated any
significant disharmony in our family and has drawn us all
closer.

I learned this principle by interviewing over a hundred

couples across the nation. I chose them initially because they seemed to have close relationships and their children, though many were teenagers, all seemed to be close to their parents and happy about it. They were enthusiastic families—radiantly happy in most instances.

When I spoke to different groups, I would scan the audience, looking for the family that seemed the happiest. Then I would interview them afterward. I often talked to the wife alone, then the husband, and finally the children. I always asked them the same questions: "What do you believe is the main reason you're all so close and happy as a family?" Without exception, each member of each family gave the same answer: "We do a lot of things together." Even more amazing to me was that all the families had *one particular activity in common.*

I can truthfully say I have tested the suggestions of these families enough to prove they are valid. I no longer fear my family will break up. Nor do I fear my children will reject my wife and me as they grow older. That's because my family is practicing the things those other successful families suggested.

Share Experiences Together

Jesus left us an example by sharing His life with the disciples. They traveled, ate, slept, healed, and ministered *together.* He guided, guarded, and kept them; then He prayed for them (John 17). His example of togetherness and oneness constantly inspires me to become "one" with my family by scheduling many times to be together.

Since every family I interviewed specifically mentioned *camping,* I looked into it as a possible recreational activity. Norma's first thought was of bugs, snakes, dirt, and all sorts of creepy-crawleys. She didn't like camping. Though I had been camping only a few times, I couldn't remember having any insurmountable problems. We decided to give it a try. Norma reluctantly agreed, frantically clutching a can of insect repellent and stuffing mosquito coils into her purse.

We borrowed a pop-tent camper and headed for Florida. We found a beautiful campsite in Kentucky, and though I was nervous being all alone in the woods, I didn't say anything. After we parked next to the only bright streetlight within fifty feet of the showers, we built a campfire to roast hot dogs and marshmallows. It was peaceful. No one was around to distract us. We put the children to bed around nine, and then Norma and I stayed up to enjoy a romantic evening. A distant thunderstorm entertained us with a light show as we enjoyed a warm breeze. Though the lightning came closer and closer, we thought it was passing to one side of us and went to bed with light hearts.

The children were asleep as I crawled into a tiny bed with Greg, and Norma joined Kari. We were lying close enough to touch hands while we whispered softly. I thought, *Boy, this is really the life. I can see why everybody likes to camp.* But my feeling of serenity was blasted away as the storm began to lash furiously around us and knocked out the streetlight beside our tent. It was pitch black except for the frequent jagged streaks illuminating the sky. Thunder rumbled, shaking the ground beneath us, and the wind began to howl. Rain beat against our tent until the water forced its way through, soaking our pillows.

"Honey, do you think this camper is going to blow over?" Norma asked faintly.

"No, not a chance," I said. I really thought the camper was going to *blow up.* I knew we were going to die. But within an hour, the storm's wrath cooled enough to let the stars shine through again. We lay there breathlessly on our soaked pillows, each wondering silently whether camping was the life for us. I was also curious as to why camping played such an important part in drawing families together. Of course, any family that faced sure death together and survived would be closer!

Colorado was the destination for our own trip in our own trailer. We could hardly wait to experience the beauty of snow-capped peaks and sniff the aroma of pine trees. I could already hear the sizzle of rainbow trout frying in the pan. As we started up the mountain, our station wagon slowed from 50 miles per hour to 30, then to 25, then to 20, until we finally slowed to the pace of 15 miles per hour. "Hot" read the temperature gauge. I felt like I was wired to the engine because my palms were sweating so. Our children sensed the tension in the air and became hyper and loud.

"I've got to stop at the next pull-off area," I told them. My nerves were frayed as I pulled over. All three kids jumped out immediately. I hadn't even had time to worry about the overheated car when our youngest, Michael, screamed at the top of his lungs.

His older brother, relieving some pent-up energy, had kicked what he thought to be an empty can. Unfortunately, it was half-full of transmission fluid. The can had landed upside down on Michael's head, and he was covered from head to toe, a terribly unhappy little boy. His nose, his ears, even his mouth were dripping with it. Not expecting such a calamity, we had no water in the trailer to clean him up. We worried that he had injured his eyes because he blinked rapidly the rest of the trip.

I've mentioned only the tragic times of our camping experiences, but we've also had tremendous experiences hiking to tops of mountains and exploring the out-of-doors. But the real significance of camping will be understood, I believe, when we get to the third point discussed in this chapter.

Doing things with your family may cost you a little extra

money, but it's worth every penny.

For example, Norma called one day to ask if I would like to buy a water-skiing boat and equipment. Though I was unsure at first, the idea seemed to appeal to everyone in the family. We purchased an "extremely experienced" model. When we were bouncing across the lake on our first time out, I noticed my wife holding on to the side as if she feared we would capsize at any moment. I thought I had everything under control, yet panic was clearly written on her face. She gripped the windshield with one hand while the other had a death grip on the bar beside her.

" Norma, what's wrong?" I questioned.

"I hate boats," she said slowly.

"You've got to be kidding. You hate boats? You're the one who called me up and said you wanted to buy the boat, and now you're telling me you hate boats? Would you like to explain that?"

I slowed our speed and let the boat idle so she could relax enough to talk to me.

"All my life I've been afraid of boats," she said. "I've just always had a real problem with boats." I sat there in total bewilderment.

She labored to explain that she hated boats, but she knew she could learn to like them. She enjoys them much more now, further convinced that boating and skiing will knit our lives together. She determined to endure boating long enough to learn to like it for the family's sake.

Not long after our first boating experience, I sat next to an executive from Boeing Aircraft on a flight to Seattle. When I asked him about his family, he told me they were very close.

"What is the most important thing that holds your family together?" I asked.

"Several years ago," he said, "we purchased a yacht and

as a family we traveled around the various inlets and islands in the Seattle area. My family enjoys boating so much that it has provided a tremendous way to knit us together."

I wish all fathers felt that way.

One man sadly admitted that when he and his children meet for a rare get-together they hardly have a thing in common.

"It's a sickening experience," he said, "to have your children back home for a visit and have nothing in common. You know, the only thing we ever laugh about as a family is when we remember the one time we took a three-week vacation. We rented a tent and camped. What a vacation! We still laugh at those experiences."

He didn't have any other fond memories of family togetherness. His wife had her women's clubs; he had his men's clubs; the children had their activities. They all grew apart in separate worlds.

"Now that my wife and I are alone, we have very little in common," he lamented. "We are two lonely people lost in our five-bedroom house."

The simple principle of sharing life together has permeated every area of our family life, from supporting Greg and Michael in soccer to supporting Kari and Greg in piano. As much as possible, we look for ways to spend time together—cooking, fishing, putting the kids to bed, gardening. Everything we do as a family assures me of our unity later in life.

When I think of a trip to Hawaii, I envision snorkeling, scuba diving, spear fishing, or anything related to being in the water. My wife thinks of an orchid lei as she steps off the airplane, dining in romantic restaurants, renting a car and sightseeing during the day. Our desires are completely different. We feel that although a husband and wife both need time to enjoy separate activities, they also need to step into the world of their mates to taste each other's interests.

While my wife is shopping, I might be snorkeling, but at night we would dine together in a very romantic place. At times my wife would want to snorkel with me, and I would enjoy sightseeing with her. I'm not saying that I would rather be touring than snorkeling or that she would rather slip on a wet suit instead of a new dress, but we believe it is important to compromise in order to share experiences. Afterwards, when the trip is only a motel receipt in your wallet, it's experiences you shared during the trip that will draw you together.

I often ask couples if they ever do things together. When I ask about vacations and the husband's face lights up while the wife grimaces, I usually conclude they took their vacation at the husband's chosen site. It was probably a dream to him and sheer torture for her and the children.

Consider the following suggestions before planning a family outing.

First, find out what activities you and your wife and your children would like to do together. Next, consider everyone's schedule to see if the planned outing will force hardship on anyone involved. For example, we agreed as a family that Greg should not be involved in group sports until this season because we felt we should be camping on weekends, instead of sitting on bleachers watching one member play football. From time to time, we adjust our schedule to make sure our family activities are not forcing one member to miss an important event.

At this point, ask your wife to name ten activities she would enjoy doing with you throughout the year.

1. _____

2. _____

3. _____

4. _____

5. _____

6. _____

7. _____

8. _____

9. _____

10. _____

Next, ask her to rate which activity of the ten is the most important to her. Don't be surprised if she prefers doing some things alone—or if she doesn't enjoy being with you at all. If she has no desire to share activities with you, reflect on your attitude toward her in the past. Have you been critical or bored? Did you pout when you had to do something she wanted to do? If so, she will remember those times and tend to avoid involvement with you in the future.

Now, let's go on to the second suggestion for becoming a close-knit family.

HE KNEW

Recognize Everyone's Need to Belong

You and I know the good feeling we have when we're able to say, "I belong to this club." "These are my friends." "The club needs my help."

During an interview with a pro-football cheerleader, I learned how much wives need to feel that sense of belonging. She told me she loved the way her husband treated her when she returned from a two-day trip. He was so excited to have her home. He pampered her, telling her how much he had missed her. But his appreciative attitude usually wore off in about two days. Then he would start taking her for granted again.

Why do we sit glued to the television as though our wives didn't exist? It seems we realize our love for them most when they're out of our lives for a few days. But after we've had them with us for a while, the "ho-hums" set in, don't they?

The principle of belonging is powerfully illustrated by an experience I had with my daughter. When Kari was nine years old, I sensed an undefined barrier between us. I couldn't detect anything specific. We just weren't close. I didn't enjoy being with her, and she didn't enjoy me either. No matter how hard I tried, I couldn't break through the barrier. From time to time, Norma would comment that I preferred my sons over my daughter. I said, "One of the reasons is because the boys are more responsive to me."

"You'd better do something to strengthen the relationship now," Norma said, "because when Kari gets older it will be much harder." So, I tested the value of belonging and decided to take Kari with me on my next seven-day business trip. Though we still weren't close, she became excited as we planned what to do and where to stay. During the plane trip we worked on her multiplication problems until it almost drove me crazy—and the man in front of us. We stayed with a farm family in Washington the first night. I noticed the rapport Kari and I felt as we laughed and sang around the dinner table with their numerous children; we were actually enjoying one another's company. At times we didn't even talk. It seemed enough just to be together. Kari seemed to have just as much fun in that farm home as she did helping me with my meetings. I let her distribute some of the material so she really felt she was a special part of my team. And she was.

We decided to take the scenic route from Portland to Seattle. I wanted to show her the small "poke and plum" town near Portland where I was raised. It's so small that by the time you "poke" your head out of the window you're "plum" out of the town. After we had a flat tire near the Columbia River, we changed it together and then walked down to the river to gather driftwood for a memento. We tried to make it up a snow-covered mountain, but had to turn around and go all the way back to Seattle the long way. We will both remember that trip, good times and bad.

I have *never* sensed a barrier between us in the years since that trip. I feel complete harmony and oneness in Kari's company. She still has the piece of driftwood sitting in her bedroom, a silent reminder of our bond and her special relationship with Christ; on it is engraved her salvation date.

Let Hard Times Draw You Together

Foxholes make lasting friendships. Haven't you heard the stories of buddies who shared the same foxhole during wartime? Whenever they meet, there is an instant camaraderie that no one can ever take away from them, a feeling born from surviving a struggle together. Trials can produce maturity and loving attitudes (James 1:2–4).

Families have foxholes too. Even when a crisis inflicts

deep scars, the dilemma can draw the family closer.

Maybe it's the crises in camping that have such a unifying effect on a family. Any family that can survive bugs, poison ivy, storms, burnt sausage, and sand in the eggs has to come out of the ordeal closer. During a crisis, you have only each other to rely on. We all look back on the mishaps that occurred during our camping trips and *laugh*, though it wasn't a bit funny at the time. Like the night Norma awakened me at two in the morning so cold that she asked, "Honey, could you take us home?" Though we were two hours from home, I abandoned my cozy bed to pack and leave. She called me her John Wayne on the way home, but at the time I didn't feel much like The Duke.

Our camping fiascos have been numerous. *Only two more hours and home sweet home*, I thought after our first camping trip. Tension electrified the air as we all longed to be home with hot water and familiar beds once again. Now when we look back on the experience we laugh, and our laughter binds us together as husband and wife and as parents and children.

THE ONE ACTIVITY THAT WIVES ENJOY THE MOST WITH THEIR HUSBANDS

Many women have told me about the importance of intimate communication with their husbands—special togetherness times—after the children are in bed, during the day on the telephone, at breakfast, at dinner, at a restaurant over a cup of coffee. These special sharing times can be the most enjoyable part of a woman's day.

My wife agrees that an intimate sharing time with me is the one thing she enjoys most about our relationship. We make it a point to have breakfast together as often as possible at a nearby restaurant just to talk about our upcoming schedules. I ask her questions about what she needs for the week and what I can do to help her and vice versa. I enjoy our discussions because I know she enjoys them. But more importantly, I would really miss those times of intimate communication if we ever neglected them.

To really understand each other during our conversations, we use a concept seldom taught in the classroom. It's called the "revolving method" of communication. Though it's very simple, you'll find it a tremendous help in avoiding misunderstandings. It involves four steps:

1. I ask my wife to share her feelings or thoughts with me.
2. I respond by rephrasing what I think she said.
3. She answers either yes or no.
4. If she answers no, I continue to rephrase what I think she said until I get a yes response.

My wife goes through the same four steps when I am explaining my feelings to her.

Our communication is more meaningful since neither of us *assumes*; we automatically know what the other is saying. (In the past, misunderstandings over implied meanings confused and ruined many discussions.) This process has nearly eliminated misinterpretations in our marriage.

FOR PERSONAL REFLECTION

1. How can Paul's example of discipleship in 1 Thessalonians 2:7–11 be applied to a family relationship?
2. Plan out a simple way to become "one flesh" (Eph. 5:31). Use the exercise below to help you.

What activities can we share together in life?

A. The Christian Life
   Church
   Prayer—when, where, how often?
   Bible study—when, where, how often?
   Witnessing
   Helping others
B. Trips or vacations
   What would our dream trip be? What would it include?
C. What are two of my favorite activities?
   Describe in detail at least one activity.
D. What are two of my wife's favorite activities?
   Is there any way to combine our favorites?
E. What is one activity in life I fear or feel inadequate to face?
   How could my mate help me overcome this fear?

11

So You Want
A Perfect Wife

"For I will not presume to speak of anything except what Christ has accomplished through me."

Romans 15:18

"If you were more submissive to me, we wouldn't have near as many problems," I used to say to my wife in a holier-than-thou voice. I was sure we would have a harmonious and fulfilling marriage if only I could motivate her to change her attitudes and responses toward me. And I was always thinking of new, creative, foolproof ways to make her change. Of course, my creative ideas usually just made her more resistant, but I didn't let that deter me. After all, most, if not all, our problems were her fault, I thought.

I even said things like, "You're so stubborn and strong-willed you're causing our marriage to decline, to deteriorate."

Or, "If only you wouldn't get so hysterical when we discuss our future plans, I would be more willing to share my life with you. I just can't tolerate your emotionalism."

I believed, at the time, that the husband was the "Captain Bligh" of the ship. When I gave the orders, I expected everyone to "snap to" and follow my leadership without offering resistance or asking questions. My distorted view made me continually critical of my wife's behavior. I can remember threatening her in a rough tone of voice to emphasize the importance of what I was saying. I gave her the silent treatment, clamming up, hoping to gain her attention so she would come crawling to me after seeing the error of her ways. And I can easily recall my persistence in lecturing her over and over again on the same issues.

Lecturing is not nearly as effective as the next three approaches.

BECOME A CONSISTENT EXAMPLE OF WHAT YOU WANT HER TO BE (ROMANS 15:18)

Studies have shown that children are much more likely to copy their parents' actions rather than their words. I have found the same principle true in adult relationships. A wife is subconsciously much more willing to emulate her husband's attitudes if they have a good relationship and she admires him. Unfortunately, the converse is true also. The more a husband demands that his wife change when he isn't a good example himself, the less desirous she is to improve herself.

I tried to change my wife in a certain area for months. I bribed her, embarrassed her, threatened not to take her on vacations, endeavoring in many "creative" ways to make her change. But the more I talked, the less she seemed to hear. I finally realized how unloving my attitude had been. I told myself I would not say another word to her about her problems until I could control myself enough to change into the tender and loving husband she needed. I was judging her in the same areas I was guilty (Rom. 2:1–2).

**HOW CAN A MAN EXPECT HIS WIFE TO GAIN
SELF-CONTROL IN AREAS OF HER LIFE WHEN
HE DOES NOT HAVE IT IN HIS OWN?**

Now *I* was ready to do some changing. "Norma, I've
been thinking of trying to change, and I'm ready to start.
I'm going to get off your back."

"You know," she said, "I've really been doing some thinking myself, and I really do want to change, especially in
that one area that bothers you."

"No, no," I said, "don't do that, because I want to be
the first to change. If you change, I won't have as much
incentive—you know how competitive I am."

"No, honey, I really want to try harder, and I'm going
to change," she replied.

I was so confused because this was the first time she had
ever been interested in changing. *Then she said something I
will never forget.*

"Gary, you know one of the reasons why it's been so
hard for me to break some of my habits? It's because your
attitude was so terrible. When you criticized me, I lost all
desire and energy to try. And you are so hateful about
criticizing me that I don't want to improve because it would
reinforce your stinky attitudes."

Now that I had taken the pressure off, she told me she
could sense the difference in my attitude. "Gary, I really
want to change, and you're really helping me now."

The Futility of Lecturing Your Wife

I learned that a husband's tender, sensitive, and understanding attitude creates far more desire within a wife than
almost anything else he can do. Unfortunately, I hadn't

learned the quality of sensitivity during our early years, and my wife did not always feel free to be completely honest with me for fear of my reactions.

A cold chill runs through me when I remember how much it hurt our marriage for Norma to feel she couldn't tell me her true feelings. One of our most painful experiences in this area began at a family reunion.

We were both tired and irritated after a long day at a family get-together near Lake Tahoe when a disagreement began. I don't know how we found enough energy to have such a fight, but it flared quite easily into an argument. I became more irritated and disturbed when she repeatedly refused to submit to me about my change of schedules. Finally her attitude bugged me so much that I told her I had had it. Here I was, on the staff of an organization that taught others how to have family harmony, and I couldn't even achieve it in my own family. I lived with an uneasy feeling that Norma might blow up at the wrong time and embarrass me. I didn't want that pressure any more, so I decided I had no choice but to quit my job and try a different type of work.

We were both so angry that evening we didn't speak. I awakened at five the next morning with a sick feeling in the pit of my stomach and walked down to the lake to think. I thought through what I would say to my boss and how I would handle the changes about to happen in my life. With a degree of peace, I walked back to the motel to tell Norma of my plans.

She began to cry, begging me not to quit my job. "I was wrong," she sobbed. "I'll change."

Her immediate change in attitude confused me.

"This time you can trust me because I guarantee you this will never happen again as long as we live," she said, still crying. "I really don't want you to quit your job because

HE KNEW

you will blame me the rest of our lives. Anything you tell me to do, I will do it."

At last, I thought, *she is beginning to see the error of her ways. Now we can get down to the business of developing a more harmonious marriage.*

I couldn't have been further from the truth. Norma had not been completely honest with me. Instead of a change of mind, she was so hurt and offended inside by my critical attitude that her heart had hardened. But since I was threatening her security, to take her away from friends and a home she loved, to move to a different location with no promise we'd even have any money, she hid her true feelings. At that time, I didn't understand how devastating such a threat could be to a woman. Norma fought to save her home the only way she knew—by giving in to me. But it wasn't because she suddenly understood my theory of marriage; it was simply that she had no alternative.

She harbored those resentful feelings for years. Consequently, our relationship could not become what it should have because of her unspoken resentment toward me. She can remember hating me on the inside but smiling on the outside. It makes me shudder to think about it. Since she appeared happy on the surface, I couldn't sense that she was inwardly disgusted with me.

As I look back on the experience today, I realize where I was at fault. I was demanding and insensitive to her needs. I made no effort to understand her physical and emotional limitations and how sudden changes affect a woman. I was also very critical of her attitudes and her fatigue. I threatened her security in a cold, calculating way. Had I been understanding enough to have waited a day or two to discuss what I wanted to do, the outcome might have been different. Only in the last few years have we developed the kind of relationship that allows this type of honesty.

DON'T DEMAND. SHARE HOW YOU FEEL

The second way to increase your wife's desire to improve your marriage is to *share* how you feel instead of demanding that she improve.

Let me clarify the "sharing" principle by breaking it down into four parts.

Learn to express your feelings through loving attitudes: warmth, empathy, and sincerity. Loving attitudes dramatically increase a woman's desire to hear your comments. Warmth is the friendly acceptance of a person, the feeling that a person is important enough for your time and effort. Empathy is the ability to understand and identify with your wife's feelings. Can you put yourself in her shoes and see the situation from her vantage point? Sincerity is showing a genuine concern for your wife both in public and at home. A comment such as, "You won't believe my old lady" gives your wife good reason to be an "old lady" when you go home.

Try to avoid using "you" statements when sharing your feelings. When you say to your wife, "You never clean up this house," or "You never have dinner on time," or "You always yell at the children," you will find she is apt to dig her heels in deeper to resist you. According to psychologist Jerry Day, "you" statements make her more determined to have her own way. When a husband says in anger, "Can't you ever think about my feelings for a change," she thinks, *His feelings! What about my feelings!* "You" statements seldom make your wife think about you; they usually infuriate her because she knows you're not concerned with her feelings.

Wait to share your feelings until your anger has subsided. When you are angry, the tone of your voice alone is likely to provoke the wrong reaction in your wife. You might even spit out words you really don't mean. While you are waiting to cool off, either remain silent or change the subject to a neutral one. If your wife asks why you are quiet, answer her honestly. Try to avoid sarcasm and say something like, "I need a little time to think this through so I can better understand my feelings." Psychologist Henry Brandt encourages a husband and wife to be honest enough to say, "I'm angry right now, and to discuss our problem would be disastrous. Could we wait until I've cooled off?" By waiting, you will be able to have a discussion instead of an argument.

Replacing "you" statements with "I feel" messages after you have both cooled down is a better way to share disagreements. Here are a few examples of what I mean:

Areas Your Wife Needs to Improve	Typical "You" Statements to Avoid	Examples of "I Feel" Messages
She doesn't respect you.	"You don't respect me like you should."	"Honey, you probably don't realize this, but I really feel discouraged whenever I hear you say disrespectful things to me." (Plug in the statement she uses that discourages you.)
She doesn't accept you the way you are.	"You're always trying to make me into somebody I'm not."	"Honey, I don't blame you for saying a lot of the things you say to me. Many times we're just not in the same world. *But I honestly don't understand many of the ways I offend you.* And I feel that you're not accepting me for who I am."
She is impatient with you.	"You never give me a chance. Would you get off my back and give me a break, I'm	"Honey, I think you deserve a gold medal for putting up with me, and I wish our relationship was better for your sake. I wish I were more

not perfect. I'm not as bad as Sarah's husband.		skilled in taking care of you, but it's probably going to take me a long time to learn these new habits. Many times I lose my desire to try when you're critical of me for not improving as fast as you wish I would."
She is critical of you in front of others.	"You make me sick when you criticize me like you did tonight. If you ever say that again I will never take you to another party. You sure made a fool of me tonight."	"Honey, I know how much you enjoy being with your friends. Would there be some time in the near future when we could talk about how I feel when we're at those parties? I hate to bring it up, but there's something you do that dampens my desire to be with our friends together. I really feel embarrassed and low when you criticize me in front of them."

Last, try to abandon "I told you so" statements. No matter how it's said, if it means "I told you so," eliminate it from your vocabulary. Such statements reflect an arrogance and self-centeredness that can be harmful to your marriage. Here are some of the more typical ways of saying "I told you so":

"If you had done what I asked you to do in the first place, this wouldn't have happened!"

"I knew it . . . just like I thought. I only asked you to do one thing . . . I can't believe that you . . . you never listen, do you? . . . See-e-e-e-e?"

"You always have to do it your way, don't you? Well, I hope you're satisfied now."

"I'm not going to say it but . . . maybe someday you'll learn to take my advice."

Can you think of any additional ways that you say to your wife, "I told you so"?

1. _____

2. _____

3. _____

4. _____

5. _____

If you can't think of any at the moment, ask your wife if she can remember some of them. Norma could.

I search out the ways I have hurt Norma's feelings, and she does the same with me. She is secure, knowing I won't *allow* her to mistreat me. She likes to be held accountable for how she makes me feel. I, too, believe it is important for a husband to have the courage to share his feelings with his wife. A lion can roar and growl, but it takes a real man to say it gently. Tell her you need comfort. Let her know you need praise. (I feel I need the same basic treatment Norma does. If she wants me to improve as a husband, it is essential that she knows what encourages or discourages me in the process.) You are the only one who can tell your wife what you need.

CREATE CURIOSITY

The third way to increase your wife's desire to improve comes from the old saying, "You can lead a horse to water but you can't make him drink." But you *can* make him drink if you put salt in his oats. The more salt you put in his oats, the greater his thirst and the more he drinks. The more curious you make your wife, the more she will want to listen. This principle has been aptly named the "salt principle." *Be stingy in sharing your feelings. Don't share them with your wife until you have her full attention.* Once you master the salt principle, you will be able to gain the attention of anyone, even when he or she knows what you are doing. Simply stated, the principle is:

NEVER COMMUNICATE YOUR FEELINGS OR IN-
FORMATION YOU CONSIDER TO BE IMPOR-
TANT WITHOUT FIRST CREATING A BURNING
CURIOSITY WITHIN THE LISTENER.

The salt principle is so powerful that I can gain the attention of my family, even if their eyes are glued to the television. If I want my children to go to bed immediately, I can use the salt principle to get them there without threats, taunts, or screams. Christ left us the example by His method of teaching and motivating people. He used parables to create interest. In fact, He advised us not to teach truth to the uninterested (Matt. 7:6).

The salt principle is so powerful that I have gotten myself into trouble using it. During a speech to a large group, someone asked a question that made me say without thinking, "Do you realize a wife can gain six attitudes that really motivate her husband to want to improve?" The moment those words left my mouth, I realized I was in trouble. A woman's hand went up. "What are those six attitudes?" she asked. I inwardly groaned as I realized I could not discuss those six attitudes and finish the topic I had started. Lowering my head, I apologized to the audience for tantalizing their curiosity. I didn't forget this salt episode because after the meeting I was mobbed by curious ladies. I can't say I felt like Burt Reynolds, but I did have to spend an hour after the meeting explaining the six attitudes. Now if you're wondering what those six attitudes are, you can find them in the companion to this book, *For Better or For Best*.

Let me use four steps to illustrate how to catch your wife's attention when you want to share your feelings.

First, clearly identify the feeling you wish to communicate to your wife. For example, you want her to understand how discouraged you become when she corrects you in public.

Second, identify some of the areas your wife wants you to change. Perhaps your wife would like you to show affection for her by holding her hand or putting your arm around her in public.

Third, use her area of high interest, salted with just a pinch of your feelings, to stimulate her curiosity. Use her high interest for affection in public and say something like, "Honey, when we're out in public or with our friends, I just want to put my arm around you and show everyone how proud I am of you. But there's something that you do occasionally that takes away my desire to hold you."

And fourth, add a little more salt by asking a short question to further arouse her curiosity. Say something like, "Do you know what you do?" Or, "I probably shouldn't say anything at this time, right?" Or, "Would you be interested in hearing what it is that causes me to feel this way?" If she isn't interested by this time, try it again later. Add a larger dose of salt to your statements.

Below are four examples of how a husband can "salt" his wife to listen to his feelings.

Area you wish your wife would change	"Salt" statements that motivate your wife to change
1. She resists your sexual advances	"Honey, do you know what really encourages me to make our marriage better? (No.) It's when I see us working together in building our marriage. (Oh, that's good.) I can think of a major area that makes me feel that you're not pulling with me. (Oh, what's that?) Is now a good time to talk about it? (Yes.) Well, I feel misunderstood and rejected when you don't respond to me at night. Could you tell me what's wrong?" (Be extra gentle and tender during the ensuing discussion. You may find out that she feels offended or any number of possibilities, but you don't have to solve the problem in one discussion.)
2. She monopolizes the conversation at parties	"Honey, I know you want to go to their home next week, but there's one thing that keeps happening when we're together that really drives me away from social gatherings in general. (Oh, what is it . . . gulp.) Well, I'm not sure I can really explain it without offending you. (Gulp, gulp.) Do you really want to talk about it? (Yes.) Well, I feel left out at parties by you." (Ask her how both of you could balance this problem. Maybe you could talk a little more and she a little less. If you discuss a plan before going to the party, you will enhance the possibility of it being more enjoyable for both of you.)
3. She doesn't want to talk when you're alone with her	"Honey, here we are again, talking about improving our relationship. You still want that, don't you? (Yes.) The best relationship possible that we can build together? (Yes.) There's one thing I don't understand that happens to us during different times of the week, and I think that it is not going to help our relationship, especially after the

children are grown and married and we're all alone. (Oh, what's that?) Well, it sort of involves the quiet times when you and I are all by ourselves and I'm really wanting to talk to you, but you don't seem to have this same desire to talk with me. I'm just wondering if there's something I'm doing that I'm not aware of, because I really want to talk with you but I don't sense that same interest in you. Maybe I'm not being sensitive to your fatigue, or whatever. I'd just like to know, because I really feel left out when you don't talk to me when we're alone."

4. She nags you about household repairs

"Honey, I don't blame you for doing one particular thing to me from time to time, because I'm sure I deserve it. But, when you say one thing to me it really causes me to lose interest in repairing things around the house. (Oh, what's that?) Well, I know it has something to do with me, and I haven't been able to figure it out yet. But in the meantime, it's not helping me to want to fix things around here. (Well, what is it? Tell me.) Maybe you can help me. Would now be a good time for you to help me figure out why you do this particular thing to me? (Yes, dear, whatever it is, let's get it out in the open and talk about it.) Well, you see, honey, I feel so unmotivated when you, sometimes in irritation or in anger, tell me five times to do something and I just can't remember to do it. As much as I want to, my mind just gets occupied with other things and I just can't remember. I really want to help around the house. How can we figure out together what needs to be done to help me get these things done and help you not to nag me about them? I feel really disinterested in doing it when you're nagging me."

In summary, if a man truly wants his wife to improve and their marriage to be strengthened, he should be the example of what he wants to see in her before saying any thing to her. He should be courageous enough to share his feelings and avoid accusing her. And finally, he should use the "salt principle" to gain her full attention before sharing his feelings.

FOR PERSONAL REFLECTION

List the changes you desire in your wife and then write out your own projects to become her example. Romans 15:18; 2:1–2.

12

Watch Out!
It Can Happen
To You

"A man's pride will bring him low, but a humble spirit will obtain honor."

Proverbs 29:23

"Norma, I really think you should take a couple of days away from the kids considering all you've faced during my absence, all the guests you had to entertain, the wedding shower, painting Greg's room. . . . I'll get a babysitter, and you just relax. I don't think you're holding up too well." I was trying to get back to work on this book, and somehow it irritated me that Norma sounded nervous and looked uptight.

She said, "I didn't need that. It makes me feel like you don't think I can handle things on my own."

"But I don't think you're handling yourself well," I said with a scowl and a harsh voice. "Surely writing a book involves more pressure than staying with the kids!"

Then the principles in my book flashed before me and broke through my irritation. I realized I was irritated and nervous and that Norma was bearing the brunt of my insensitivity. I had blown it again!

"You're right. You didn't need that. You *are* doing great. When will I ever learn?"

The next morning she came over to my hideaway motel for breakfast, and we again discussed how I had missed a chance to encourage her. My motives were to help, but my insensitive words came out of a doubt that I *really* was the kind of husband I should be. If I were the right kind of husband, maybe my wife wouldn't have to feel so nervous and rundown. My thoughts had been, *Honey, only a week and I'll be finished with both books. Please hang on. What will people think of my book if you don't look like I'm making you happy?*

Norma said she understood and reminded me that my offensive behavior comes less and less often, that the periods of disharmony get shorter and shorter as we learn how to restore our relationship.

Why are those hard times fading away? Two reasons:

1. I *admit* my offensive ways and quickly accept the fact that I haven't arrived.
2. I *earn* her forgiveness sooner by following the ideas in chapter 5.

(And we are *both reaching* for the best possible relationship. That helps a lot!)

"But," you ask, "when can I relax and enjoy the fruit of my labor?"

Do you remember the story of the young couple who separated for a year until the husband learned how to regain his wife's affection? (See chapter 2.) She couldn't live with his lazy, insensitive, dominant, selfish mannerisms.

He followed many of the principles shared in this book for five years after they reunited, and she was regaining a romantic love and starting to blossom. Then he made the *big mistake! He relaxed and wanted a little return for his years of effort.* He assumed that now he could start enjoying the fruit of his labor. He slowly reverted to his old habits and attitudes: lazy, insensitive, dominant, selfish. Once again she started to lose her feelings of love for him.

Today he is starting all over again. Fortunately, this time they both desire a better marriage and both are seeking help as a couple.

Building a successful marriage is a lifelong endeavor.

Don't relax! And never assume that you've arrived! Pride always comes before a fall (Prov. 29:23)!

Or, you say, "I'm tired of starting all over again."

One man couldn't stick with it. He kept forgetting some of the principles shared in this book. His wife was ready to leave him, and nothing seemed to help, until one day I said to him, "Jim, each time you fail to comfort her and each time you lose your temper, you're back to the starting block in her mind—at that point she still wants to leave you."

"That does it," he said. "No way am I going to keep starting all over again." *And he didn't.* That was the end of his angry outbursts.

You may take great strides forward, but each time you slip, your wife may think you haven't changed a bit. Remember, it took my wife two years to believe me.

FOR PERSONAL REFLECTION

1. How does the secret of prayer relate to becoming a more consistently loving husband?

> Luke 11:5–8—the secret is in verse 8.
> Luke 18:1–7—the secret is in verse 5.

2. How many times should a husband forgive his wife and keep trying to build a loving marriage? Matthew 18:21–22.

Resources

Brandt, Henry, with Landrum, Phil. *I Want My Marriage To Be Better*. Grand Rapids, Michigan: Zondervan Publishing House, 1976.

Collins, Gary. *How To Be a People Helper*. Santa Ana, California: Vision House Publishers, 1976.

Day, Jerry. Clinical Psychologist, Tucson, Arizona: Ideas on stress management.

Dobson, James. *What Wives Wish Their Husbands Knew About Women*. Wheaton, Illinois: Tyndale House Publishers, Inc., 1975.

Drescher, John M. *Seven Things Children Need*. Scottdale, Pennsylvania: Herald Press, 1976.

Gothard, Bill. Director and lecturer, from the Institute in Basic Youth Conflicts. Oakbrook, Illinois.

Hardisty, Margaret. *Forever My Love*. Irvine, California: Harvest House Publishers, 1975.

Hendricks, Howard. *What You Need to Know About Premarital Counseling*. Waco, Texas: Family Life Cassettes, Word, Inc.

Hockman, Gloria. "A New Way for Families to Solve Problems Together." *Family Weekly*, July 16, 1978, p. 6.

Jones, Charles. *Life Is Tremendous*. Wheaton, Illinois: Tyndale House Publishers, 1968.

LaHaye, Tim and Beverly. *The Act of Marriage*. Grand Rapids, Michigan: Zondervan Publishing House, 1970.

LaHaye, Tim. *Understanding the Male Temperament*. Old Tappan, New Jersey: Fleming H. Revell Company, 1977.

Nair, Ken. *Discovering the Mind of a Woman*. Laredo, Texas: Fiesta Publishing Co., 1982.

Osborne, Cecil G. *The Art of Understanding Your Mate*. Grand Rapids, Michigan: Zondervan Publishing House, 1970.
Wheat, Ed. Family Physician, Springdale, Arkansas: Tapes on sex in marriage: "Sex Technique and Sex Problems in Marriage," and "Love-Life for Every Married Couple."

Resources By Gary Smalley

The Blessing, co-authored with Dr. John Trent. Nashville, Tennessee: Thomas Nelson Publishers, 1986.

Many people spend a lifetime searching for their parents' love and acceptance—their "blessing." *The Blessing* looks at the powerful Old Testament concept of "blessing children" as a tool to help our *children* in the present and to help *us* deal with emotional hurts of the past.

For Better or For Best. Grand Rapids Michigan: Zondervan Publishing House, 1979, Revised Edition, 1987.

This book is written just for the wife. Discover practical ways a wife can help to strengthen her marriage and all her important relationships.

The Gift of Honor, co-authored with Dr. John Trent. Nashville, Tennessee: Thomas Nelson Publishers, 1987.

Whether we realize it or not, the degree that we value God, others, and ourselves greatly determines the success or failure of all our relationships. Learn what it means to "honor" God and our loved ones and how to avoid the incredible damage that can come from "dishonoring" them.

If Only He Knew. Grand Rapids, Michigan: Zondervan Publishing House, Revised Edition, 1987.

A valuable guide to helping a husband learn how to understand and love his wife in a meaningful way. The companion volume to *For Better or For Best*.

Joy That Lasts. Grand Rapids, Michigan: Zondervan Publishing House, 1986.

A personal glimpse into Gary's life as he shares insights from his experience and from the Scriptures—insights that

193

and other negative emotions and replace them with love, peace, and joy.

The Key to Your Child's Heart. Waco, Texas: Word Books, 1984.

Practical parenting methods which have been featured on Dr. Jim Dobson's radio program, "Focus on the Family," including "opening your child's spirit," family contracting, and becoming a close-knit family.

The "Love is a Decision" film series. Grand Rapids, Michigan: Zondervan Corporation.

A six-part film series where Gary goes through six principles on developing loving and lasting relationships. Your church or study group can order the film series through your local Christian film distributor or by calling Zondervan at 1–800–233–3480.

For additional information about Gary's books, his national speaking schedule, or to order the audio-cassette tapes of his "Love is a Decision" film series, please write:

Today's Family
P.O. Box 22111
Phoenix, Arizona 85028

Gary Smalley teaches seminars throughout North America on marriage and the family. Among his books are: FOR BETTER OR FOR BEST, THE JOY OF COMMITTED LOVE, and JOY THAT LASTS.